Your CLASSROOM or Their PLAYGROUND

CLASSROOM MANAGEMENT OBSERVATIONS AND CONVERSATIONS FOR THE NEW TEACHER

IANTHA USSIN, MAT

This book is dedicated to the first class I ever loved.

Homeroom 208

"The Family"

2007-2008

Tubman Middle School

Augusta, GA

"If teachers can't manage their classrooms, they can't offer their students effective instruction.
It just doesn't work."

— Ms. Ussin

Contents

Foreword

Why do you want to be a teacher? This is the probing question that sets the stage for the start of every 2000-level class every semester for my undergraduate students. Though a challenge, I find it necessary to boldly share the ins and outs of what it takes to be an effective teacher; I'm not afraid to share with students the need for a change of major if their disposition does not present a true desire for enlightening and cultivating young minds.

Nevertheless, my probing question is followed with: Who were your worst teachers? Why? Who were your best teachers? Why? I like to start this way for two reasons: (1) to help my undergraduate students reflect upon and understand their own experiences as students (K-12) and (2) to aid in their understanding and developing of the experiences they intend to create for their students (K-12).

Without fail, each semester and in every class, there is ample sharing regarding the teachers that my undergraduate students deemed as the worst. A common trend in answers always seems to follow along the ideas that "my teachers didn't care, my teachers were mean, and my teachers didn't connect with me."

Now it's my time. At this point, I am in full Professor Mode! My students have just armed me with the tools necessary to break the mold towards making a better public school experience for students to come. After all, I love teaching teachers to be great teachers!

As a former Middle Grades Science Educator, I share countless experiences of what it is like to navigate student personalities, behaviors, cultural differences, and learning styles. The one practice that allows all the magic to happen is… classroom management.

When I think of the word "management," I think of an organized, well-structured and functioning entity with supervisors and subordinates. The manager conducts progress monitoring, provides opportunities for team-building, and publicly acknowledges those who excel. Just like the manager of any organization or business, an effective teacher must fulfill all these tasks in order to properly manage the classroom. Although the above sounds like a great day in the office, like the classroom, it has its challenges.

Let's take a look.

Imagine you're fully enveloped in teaching the most exciting lesson of your career with students all tuned in and engaged, only to be continuously disrupted…not by a student in your class, not by someone from the office on the intercom…but by the teacher next door. On this particular day, neither I nor my students could get the full essence of the day's lesson because the teacher was yelling at students every five minutes. I quickly ran over when the first explosion took place, thinking that something was terribly wrong. I expected to see students everywhere, objects flying, and the teacher backed into a corner. To my surprise, all of his students were seated in their desks, talking and "off-task," of course, but I seemed to not find what the issue was to warrant such a response.

Guess what? The issue, as explained by the teacher, was the TALKING! "Are you serious?" is what I was thinking.

Like my probing question, I share this experience every semester during my Classroom Management course to gauge my students' perspective on why this teacher was "dealing" with his students in this manner as opposed to managing them. You guessed it! My students always start with, "It doesn't seem like he has a connection with the students." This is the answer that I look for every semester. If a teacher does not seek to make some kind of connection with each of his/her students, classroom management is not a practice, only a theory.

This book is a must in the hands and toolkits of every pre-service and new teacher. It serves as a classroom management manual for the operation of one of the most significant mechanisms of society—the K-12 classroom. Riddled with how to put the parts together and what causes the mechanism to fail, *Your Classroom or Their Playground* includes time-proven and research-based practices that pre-service and new teachers need to effectively cultivate and enlighten the young minds of tomorrow.

Dr. Chaundra R. Creekmur
Assistant Professor
College of Education
Savannah State University

Introduction

I spent a considerable amount of time thinking of some clever way to open this book. I wanted to grab your attention in a way that made me appear super teachery. You just had to know, from my very first words, that I was credible. I was determined. There were quite a few episodes of putting the introduction down for days at a time to let it breathe and revisiting it after its rest period to try again. Then, one day, I remembered something major. When the idea for this book was first conceived, I contracted with myself to be candid, through and through, from the first to the last page. In agreeing to put pen to paper and release every thought, scenario, and piece of advice I believed would be beneficial for new teachers, I vowed to be raw. I promised to be real. I thought back to the discussions I had with some of my colleagues about the premise of the book and surmised once again, as we did after every "book chat," that my experiences and the wisdom I gained from 15 years of teaching make me just as credible as any of the other authors whose classroom management books I've read.

I've seen a lot.

I've experienced a lot.

I've learned a lot.

And now, I have a lot to share.

It's my truth and transparency and the barefaced peek inside my classroom and the schools where I've taught—every good, bad, and ugly event—that makes this a worthy read for every teacher candidate and beginning teacher. In fact, it should be a required text. An audacious declaration, I admit, but on it, I stand firm.

In the thirteen chapters that follow, I initiate conversations by uncovering personal experiences and key observations from my tenure as a classroom teacher. You get to carry on the conversation with a personal reflection at the end of each chapter. Our time together will commence with my showing you what not to do in your classroom. Then you'll have a Planning Period to digest it all. After that, we'll continue our talk with what you *should* do in your classroom if you plan for it to be well-managed and conducive to learning, because one thing I know is this: Every teacher gets the option of having a classroom or settling for a playground. My prayer is for this book to save you from having the latter. Let this instructive body of work be a tool in your box of teacher tips and tricks that assists in establishing an environment where you and your students can experience, daily, the wonder of learning.

If you're reading this and you've been newly hired as a teacher, welcome to the education profession! No other work is as uniquely challenging as ours, but none as rewarding either.

May I help you lessen some of the challenges and see more of the rewards?

Let's dive into the conversation.

Section 1

Taking Notes

Chapter 1

Are You Being You?

Be yourself; everyone else is already taken.

-Oscar Wilde

The Warm-Up / Bell Ringer

Students can smell a fake, and they can smell that fake a mile away. It seems every student has an uncanny, intuitive ability to know if a teacher is trying to be someone s/he's not. It's like a special sixth sense. They just know.

Students know if a teacher doesn't care about them, and they know if a teacher has their best interest at heart. They know if a teacher is concerned for their academic success, and they know if a teacher is teaching simply because it's their job. They know if a teacher is skilled and able to teach them, and they know if a teacher doesn't know what the heck they're doing.

Students just know.

And contrary to what many may think, students don't require much. They're simple—the kindergartener, the high school senior, and every student in between. They want to know you care, they want quality, engaging instruction, and they want you to be you. That's it. It won't matter if you're strict, as long as you care. They won't be bothered by how much work you assign, as long as you're making the curriculum interesting. They won't care if you're quirky, as long as you're owning that that's who you really are. They'll thank you later for being strict and helping them grow in discipline. Later, they'll express gratitude for the challenging assignments that taught them what it means to work hard. And your quirkiness, or whatever quality is most you, will eventually be what they love most about you.

Ms. Gruwell (Ms. G.), the main character in the movie *Freedom Writers*, is a perfect example of what it means to be oneself. She, a naively optimistic and stereotypically suburban, Caucasian first-year teacher, accepted a position teaching freshman and sophomore English at a racially divided, gang-infested high school in Long Beach, California. At Woodrow Wilson High, race was against race, but every race was against White people, and because of this, before even getting to know Ms. G., her Black, Hispanic, and Asian students wrote her off as the enemy. As if simply being White wasn't enough to form the natural divide between her and her students, Ms. G.'s prim and proper misuse of street vernacular had the potential to widen the gap even further. But it didn't. In fact, it closed the gap.

Ms. G. didn't know the slang. She wasn't privy to what to say or how to say it, so when she attempted and failed each time, it was pure comedy for the students, making her appear even more lame than they had already pegged her to be. Later, though, surprisingly, it was what tethered the students to her. Ms. G. being Ms. G. was what helped build the relationship bridge with her students and what later formed a family atmosphere in her classroom. She didn't change her mess-ups; she just let them be. She didn't try harder to "get it right" to "be like them." She just let herself be. The students knew she wasn't capable of miraculously stripping herself of everything that made her the unique Ms. G. she was—her God-given personality and the upbringing and life experiences that shaped her walk and her talk. But they wanted to see her, the polar opposite of everything they were, stumble with every attempt to somehow relate to them. It made them like her more because she was—say it with me now—just being Ms. G. They anticipated her snafus and eventually, instead of meeting them with judgement and criticism, welcomed the mess-ups and welcomed the super duper White Ms. G. into their anti-White world. And isn't that how relationships work? A whole bunch of me accepting you and you accepting me, completely, for everything we are, quirks, flaws, mess-ups and all? It's quite endearing.

In middle and high schools, and some elementary schools where there is change of classes throughout the school day, students are accustomed to seeing different teachers and actually expect their teachers to be different. Students want order, rules, and expectations to be the same across the board, but they anticipate teachers being unique in the way they execute them. They understand no two teachers are exactly alike, and they know teachers will simply be who they are and do things the way they do.

Work Session: Ms. Ussin's Story

When I taught 6th grade, I had a catchy call-and-response clap that I used to get my students' attention when it was time to end station activities or group work sessions. It pulled us all back together on the same silent sheet of music to receive instructions for next steps or to make an orderly transition to what we already knew was next. I used the clap regularly in my classroom, of course, but one school year, I found myself using it a few times in the hallway during our team's class change and in a grade-level assembly with school administrators too. My clap was no secret, and it wasn't intended to be, but it was designed to be what only Ms. Ussin used for the students that year. It was our thing.

One day, I heard one of the teachers on my team, Ms. Duplicate, using the clap to get the students in order in her classroom. I had to do a double take. I was shocked! I had never heard my signature clap ring out with any other adult hands. At first, I thought, *"Okay, it's obvious Ms. Duplicate wanted to use it because she's seen it work, specifically, with our students. It was effective in calling them to order. Cool. Quick fix. I get it."* But after a week or so, I heard the clap bouncing off the walls in her room more often. Too often, in fact. It was being used, some days, four and five times in the span of only a few minutes, and that wasn't how it was supposed to be used. Maybe when she employed it at first, it had some effect, but it wasn't long at all before its purpose and power fizzled in her room.

When my students were quietly working on a quiz one Friday afternoon, I decided to stop the work I was doing at my desk and listen to the rousing activity that was underway down the hall in Ms. Duplicate's classroom. I heard students talking and laughing and moving about the room as Ms. Duplicate was in the middle of instruction. Ms. Duplicate clapped the clap, and the class responded by repeating the clap back to her. When silence filled the room, she continued to teach, but soon thereafter, the noise stirred up again. Ms. Duplicate clapped the familiar rhythm again, but that time, there were fewer students to respond. Some clapped, but others continued to talk. Ms. Duplicate attempted to continue instruction, but the students, at that point, were fully engaged in their own conversations and activities. They were done listening. Ms. Duplicate then did what almost caused me to stop using the clap altogether. She proceeded to repeat that clap, continually, for about seven rounds, until a few students started saying, "Y'all, just clap so she can stop clapping."

It was obvious the students were tired of hearing it. I, too, had grown weary of hearing its voice. I knew if they had developed that attitude toward the clap with Ms. Duplicate, it could happen with me too, even though with me, in my room, it was home. That clap was ours, something the students once loved, but it had officially been milked and zapped of its personal pizzazz. It had been taken by someone who didn't know how to use it, and because she wasn't clear on its proper execution, she abused it.

Author and Christian minister, Dr. Myles Munroe once said, "Where the purpose of a thing is not known, abuse is inevitable," and that was the case with the clap. Ms. Duplicate abused the attention-getting tool because it didn't originate with her. She didn't fully understand its purpose. She didn't know it was to be used only with two or three classroom activities, and even then, used sparingly.

After that, I would use the clap only in high times of need when we were well into group activities that required a considerable amount of movement in the room. I noticed the students responded about the same as before because Ms. Ussin was the one making the call. After a while, though, I just couldn't bear to use it anymore because I knew they'd be hearing it continually down the hall, hating every beat of the clap.

And sure enough, because kids are kids, different ones would say things like, "Ms. Ussin, Ms. Duplicate be using yo clap." And others would chime in with, "Yup! But she don't use it right."

I would just think, *"Yeah. I know."*

The Closing / Lesson Wrap-Up

You see, we can have the same tools, but the one of us who doesn't know how to use them won't get the results that the one who knows how to use them will. This is why it's best to bring your own tools—the ones you're most familiar with—to your classroom. No one can work those tools like you.

I can go and buy all of the same things the seamstress buys—the thread, the buttons, the fabric, and the patterns, but if I don't know how to work a sewing machine, I won't get the pretty dress in the end. I'm not a seamstress; the seamstress and I won't have the same results. What I can do, though, is get the jewelry to match the dress. I know jewelry.

Pairing jewelry with clothing comes naturally for me. So, when the seamstress—you, Ms. Math Teacher—presents the dress that was made with the expert use of your tools, and I—Ms. English Teacher—add the jewelry to complement the dress, using my tool of expert coordination, our customer—the student—is completely satisfied, well dressed, and quite dashing!

We both make the customer happy and give her something she needs, but I do it being the me I was created to be, and you do it being you. We both employ our own tools. And guess what? The customer always looks to us for our specific strengths and enjoys getting something different from each of us. She never seeks me out for a dress and never goes to you for jewelry.

So, I ask… Are you being you? Are you using your unique gifts, skills, talents, and ideas and implementing those things into your lessons, activities, and routines? Ultimately, that's what your students want. They want to see you being you.

The Experts Agree

The goal is not to create some kind of cookie-cutter teacher that everyone should mold into. The best teachers are those who let their personalities show in their classrooms. Teachers who try to be someone else are asking for serious problems. Having to "fake it" too much will eventually wear a teacher out.

Discipline without Anger:
A New Style of Classroom Management, 2012
Doug Campbell (the Discipline Doctor)

Homework

When you think about how you want to "show up" in your classroom and how you want your students to "see you," what comes to mind? What is one takeaway from this chapter that encourages you to be the teacher you see in your mind?

Reflect.

_____

_____

_____

_____

_____

_____

_____

_____

_____

_____

Chapter 2

I'm Not Ms. Eclair!

You never look good trying to make someone else look bad.

-Author Unknown

I'M NOT MS. ECLAIR!

The Warm-Up / Bell Ringer

Students complained all year that Ms. Eclair didn't teach. They said she'd tell them what to do, but she wouldn't necessarily teach them how to do it. Her class, they said, was more of a "do the work" class, and that there was plenty of work to be done that never got graded. Students were frustrated, and parents regularly expressed their displeasure with Ms. Eclair and her seeming inability to give their children what they were supposed to receive from her class.

Students eventually learned that they could do what they wanted to do, as long as the work was done, however they decided to do it, since it probably wouldn't be assessed for accuracy anyway. Students would walk out of Ms. Eclair's classroom when she wasn't looking, and later return just as inconspicuously as they'd left. They would erase important notes and reminders from the board, swearing that nothing had been on the board when their class entered the room. They'd say the board had to have been erased before they arrived. They even went as far as ensuring that sets of books and assignments for the class, graded and ungraded, mysteriously disappeared. It was hard to watch the shenanigans unfold, day in and day out. There was always something. Her room was a playground, and the students were having a ball! And Ms. Eclair, bless her heart, didn't have a clue. She really didn't. Honestly.

None of this, however, is why I'm introducing her to you. It's Mr. Magnificent, her next-door neighbor and teammate, who brings her to light. It is he who made her already-struggling classroom management go from about a C+ (every day wasn't a mess) to an F. You don't ever want to find yourself becoming a Mr. Magnificent.

Work Session: Ms. Ussin's Story

That year, more than any other, whenever my planning period would allow, and sometimes even when it didn't, I loved visiting other teachers' classrooms to watch them teach. I delighted in seeing different strategies others were using and observing how their classrooms flowed.

One day, after stopping in on one of Mr. Magnificent's math lessons, I knew it wouldn't be my last visit. I had never seen math taught quite the way he taught it. His instruction caused concepts I'd learned way back in junior high school to come right back to mind, and with ease. Although my junior high and high school math teachers were amazing and sent me away as a full-fledged math scholar, I had to admit that Mr. Magnificent's teaching helped me see geometry in a whole new way. I remember being so caught up in the lesson that I'd forgotten about time. I'd spent most of my 75-minute planning period in his class! I was so impressed...so engaged...and way too interested in seeing if I'd gotten the right answer to a practice problem. Mr. Magnificent's classroom had order. The students were totally tuned in, and even more than their being actively engaged in what they were learning, they were completely in control of it.

When I walked in about 20 minutes into the class period, there were work session instructions on the board for what each person at each table should be doing and a second set of instructions to guide them through a series of word problems at their tables. If students were assigned to be ones at their tables, they had one job. If students were twos at their tables, they had a different job, and so on. Mr. Magnificent walked around the classroom to monitor students for the first 10 minutes as they worked on the first problem. Then, when the 10 minutes had passed, he went to the board and walked through the steps students should've taken with the problem. If students had messed up, they knew exactly where and how, and they were able to self-assess and self-correct.

After that mini lesson, students went on to the next word problem just like the one they'd done before. This time, they had to show they could walk through the same steps Mr. Magnificent had just modeled. They were given a new problem with more challenging numbers, of course, and as Mr. Magnificent put it, "a funky fraction." The students were eager to get it right; they wanted to impress Mr. Magnificent and make him proud. They challenged each other at their tables, and they even challenged among tables. I could hear some of the macho boys saying things like, "I bet you won't get this one right," and "How much you wanna bet I get this one done before you?" Oh, it was a joy to watch! There was no doubt that Mr. Magnificent was truly magnificent.

Until he wasn't.

A couple weeks after that class visit, I decided to drop in again and catch Mr. Magnificent's class from the beginning. I wanted to see how he greeted students and how he opened his lessons. I was interested to learn how students entered the classroom and what their rituals and routines were. I walked the halls with the students during class change, and as the tardy bell rang, I walked right into Mr. Magnificent's class and took a seat.

Mr. Magnificent was finishing something at his desk from the previous class period. I could see him stacking papers and organizing his desk. He was tossing a "Good Morning" here and there as students passed his desk to get to their seats, but he never stopped the work he was doing. When students walked in, they didn't hesitate to get right to work on the Bell Ringer Activity that was projected on the Promethean board. Most of the class was already knee deep into a word problem after having been in their seats for only about two minutes. They had shut the world out around them. There were about four students, however, who were acting as if that day was their first day in Mr. Magnificent's class. Two young men had not yet taken their seats, and they were standing next to two other guys who were in their seats looking up talking to them. They had formed an almost circle and whatever they were talking about must have been hilarious. It was so funny that it caused Mr. Magnificent to look up from what he was doing with what I could tell was a familiar glare in his eye. Without his even saying a word, the boys who were standing scrambled to their seats. One boy tripped over a book bag which caused him to topple into his seat, and that only made matters worse because the class erupted with laughter.

Mr. Magnificent just stood at his desk and looked at the boy. He shook his head and waited for the class's giggles to simmer. When the young man finally got his notebook atop the desk, and when his pencil finally began to shakily creep across his paper, Mr. Magnificent spoke. But he didn't speak directly to the young man. Instead, he addressed the entire class. He said, "I don't know how many times I'm gon' have to tell y'all... I am NOT Ms. Eclair! If you don't know how to come in here and do what you're supposed to do, you can do it at home. This is Mr. Magnificent's class, not Ms. Eclair's. We don't roll like that in here."

I couldn't believe what I was hearing! I thought I would die! Had he really just pulled the rug from under his teammate? Had he really just added insult to injury by pouring salt on an open wound? Yes, and yes. He most certainly had!

The Closing / Lesson Wrap-Up

I don't know about you, but where I'm from, the teachers I work with don't play that "talk about another teacher in students' presence" game. In all my years of teaching, it was clear, across the board, that we just weren't having that in our classrooms. We didn't have to be the best of friends or even get along for that matter, but we respected each other when we were before our students.

I remember a specific instance with one of my teams. We had just had a disagreement in a morning meeting before the school day started. Our meeting ended right as the morning bell rang for students to enter the building. As we welcomed students into our homeroom classes that day, there was no sign of the discord on any of our faces or in our demeanor. The students never knew it, and we made sure of it. The whole day was like any other—business as usual.

One of the things I would share with my students on the first or second day of school every year is, "If you have something bad to say about another teacher, keep it to yourself when you're in my classroom because I can assure you I'm not about to let you talk about ner' one of my teammates up in here."

And that's a wrap. I've hardly ever had to address the "talk about other teachers" issue because every year, my students know I mean business where that's concerned.

In my saying that to the students, what I was really communicating was...

1. Talking about others is not right. Follow my example.
2. This is a positive learning environment. Keep it that way.
3. I'm a professional adult.

YOUR CLASSROOM OR THEIR PLAYGROUND

4. Your other core teachers and I are a team, and you can't play us against each other. If you try, it won't work.

Without saying it directly, Mr. Magnificent was conveying some messages too.

1. It's okay to talk about others if it makes you look good. Follow my example.
2. Do what you're supposed to do in this learning environment. Do whatever you want to do in other teachers' classrooms. You don't have to have character, and your behavior doesn't have to be consistent throughout the school.
3. I take my professionalism off every now and then. Follow my example.
4. Your other core teachers and I aren't a team. You can break our walls down whenever you want. Try it. It'll work.

Know this: There will be many battles to fight in this profession, and your teammates and co-workers are your allies on the battlefield. In a school, no man is an island. Your teacher friends should become like family if you're "allying" right. You don't have to face issues with difficult students and parents alone, but you will if you pull a Mr. Magnificent. If your administrators aren't supportive, you don't have to face that alone either. You can have the loving support of your team and co-workers if you don't pull a Mr. Magnificent. We're in it together. We need each other. Embrace your colleagues, and enjoy the strength that comes from unified camaraderie.

Even if Ms. Eclair wanted to dig her way out of the dog house with her students and start a whole new way of doing things, her credibility and any chance she would ever have to do so was shot to the ground. The students would always hear the voice of the teacher they love and respect over the one whose classroom they deemed to be a playground. Ms. Eclair was never able to earn their respect. The students did just what Mr. Magnificent told them to do (even though he didn't say it directly): Behaved themselves in his class and "went to the playground" in hers.

What a shame!

The Experts Agree

A school is a community within a community. You will want to establish productive, positive, and professional relationships with your administrator, colleagues, other staff, and support providers. Good working relationships can make or break the school year.

The Teacher's Guide to Success, **2008**
Dr. Ellen L. Kronowitz

Teachers would be wise to never name names of other people at the school for any reason publicly. This goes for teachers, students, and other school employees.

Discipline without Anger:
A New Style of Classroom Management, **2012**
Doug Campbell (the Discipline Doctor)

"Think before you speak" is one of the best pieces of advice a leader can internalize. The best leaders take the time to look at every decision with care, commitment, and connections—how will it affect others?

If You Don't Feed the Teachers, They Eat the Students!
Guide to Success for Administrators and Teachers, **2010**
Dr. Neila A. Connors

Homework

Have you ever been thrown under the bus by someone who was "on your team?" How did it feel? Have you ever witnessed it happening to someone else? Do you agree with the opening thought for this chapter: *"You never look good trying to make someone else look bad?"*

Reflect.

_____

_____

_____

_____

_____

_____

_____

_____

_____

_____

Chapter 3

Save the Yelling For the Game

A harsh word stirs up anger; a gentle answer turns away wrath.

- Proverbs 15:1, *The Holy Bible*

The Warm-Up / Bell Ringer

"Ms. Ussin, can we close our door?"

My students had just finished a three-station group rotation and it was time for them to independently analyze the information their groups had discovered together. It was quiet. They were deep into their work, and I, who made it a point to steal away and tackle administrative duties whenever my students were silently "checked out," was in my zone. I must've been totally immersed in whatever I was doing that day because it wasn't until I responded to my student's question with my own query that I heard why the class wanted the door closed.

"Why do we need the door closed?"

On came the litany of responses.

"Because they are soooo loud down there."

"Oh my God! I can't even think."

"And he keep on hollerin', 'Shuuut uuuuup!'"

They all burst into laughter at the last comment that was accompanied by one of their classmate's always-accurate impression of the teacher down the hall. I could hear them inside their lingering giggles with more comments.

"That's all he do is holler."

"I don't even wanna go down there today."

"Dion, close the door. You the closest to it."

I hushed all the hubbub in the room and reminded them about my policy on talking about other teachers. I nodded to Dion to go ahead and close the door because they were right. It was football-stadium loud down there, and it was echoing in the hallway. The door being closed only muffled the noise; we still heard it all.

As the students down the hall were having a party, it seemed, all we would hear from Mr. Redfield, over and over, is "Shuuut uuuuuuuuup!" After his plea, each time, there would be a thunderous upheaval of mockery, wild, gut bustin', knee slappin' chuckling, and the like, directed at Mr. Redfield. Then, things would die down for a minute, but not long after, they'd be up again—the rollercoaster, true to its nature, full of cheers and screams.

Even my students laughed when they heard, "Sit DOWN! Michael! I saaaid, SIT DOOOOWN!" Everybody knew Michael and that he lived for making Mr. Redfield yell.

The students knew they were winning. They knew what buttons to push to set that class ablaze every day, and they would team up to push them as often as an opportunity allowed. They intentionally got Mr. Redfield to "blow the roof" so they could laugh.

Dissimilarly, Ms. Calgon, the epitome of a gentle and quiet spirit, in over 20 years of teaching (five of which I witnessed), never once raised her voice with her students.

Work Session: Ms. Ussin's Story

I'll never forget the day I first saw Ms. Calgon work her quiet magic.

As teachers stood at their doors during class changes, we'd sometimes venture to a neighbor teacher's door if it was in eyeshot of our own. Ms. Calgon's room was diagonally across from mine that year, so she and I would often visit each other to talk. She could still see her class from my door, and I could see mine from hers.

One fall morning, on Tacky Day of our school's Spirit Week, our students were unusually hyper. The hallways were vibrating with raucous that was on a level we hadn't seen all year, and because students don't always know where to draw the line, they walked that excitement from the bustling hallway right into Ms. Calgon's class.

I knew, from talking to her as much as I had all year, sharing teaching strategies and ideas, that students routinely walked into her room, read the board for what she called "First Things First," and followed the written instructions to complete whatever warm-up activity she'd prescribed. When her students didn't do that that day—the very thing they'd done every day since the second week of school—Ms. Calgon was befuddled. She couldn't believe what she was seeing, and she was definitely taken aback at what she was hearing.

In her usual gentle way, Ms. Calgon just barely touched me on my shoulder, and with her endearing smile, politely interjected a whispery "Excuse me, Ms. Ussin." In the smallest, sweetest voice, she then said, "I think we'll have to pick this up a little later."

I watched Ms. Calgon take the daintiest four or five steps from my door to hers, with her arms crossed behind her back and her hands loosely locked. Once she reached her room, she stood at the threshold, arms still crossed, hands still locked. She peered into the classroom and watched the students who were standing at each other's desks, conversing and jigging about.

After observing at the door for a few seconds, she pressed her left shoulder into the door frame and leaned in with all her weight, as if to say, *"I'm just gonna rest here a while."* Soon, the students began to notice that Ms. Calgon was standing at the door watching them behave diametrically contrary to what they'd been taught.

Slowly, one by one, after making abashed and slightly terror-stricken glances at the door, students began to take their seats. Once seated, they all speedily grabbed their notebooks and pens and pencils and gave full, laser-focused attention to "First Things First." There was complete silence in the room not even two minutes after Ms. Calgon sashayed from my room and asserted her mere presence at the threshold of her door. It seemed like seconds!

Ms. Calgon's students had the reverential fear for her that one has for someone or something they profoundly honor and respect. Their panicked scuttles to their assigned seats and quick readjustments to "the regularly scheduled program" was an act of veneration. They wanted Ms. Calgon to know that they knew they'd messed up, and they wanted her to know they knew how to fix it without her having to say a word. They were embarrassed, and they knew Ms. Calgon knew they were. There was mutual understanding all around. Ms. Calgon knew they carried their shame on their shoulders, and that load was heavy enough. She didn't add any more weight by giving the students a lecture or by singling anyone out. She simply stood at the door for maybe another minute, shoulder still pressed in the door frame, while the students worked. When she was ready to review "First Things First," she peeled herself from her stance and walked into the thick silence that permeated the room. The students had learned their lesson, and I can attest that I personally didn't witness another episode of that sort with her class again all school year.

The Closing / Lesson Wrap-Up

Think back to Mr. Magnificent. He just looked at his students, and the unacceptable behavior came to a screeching halt. Ms. Calgon's presence alone was the only management tool she needed in that instance (and many others I wish I had time to detail). In both scenarios, the students were just as much in control as the teacher. There was no need for the teacher to even speak, so certainly, there was no need to yell. The students knew what their teachers expected of them. It was apparent that classroom rituals and routines had been established and put into daily practice, and because students knew what was expected and knew their teacher would hold them accountable, they did what was expected. And students, for the most part, want to make their teachers proud and please them in this way. *Your* students want to make you proud in this way.

Mr. Redfield didn't set many expectations for his students the first couple weeks of school, so the rest of his school year was unnecessarily tough. There were no daily routines—no set way for students to walk into the classroom, no starting activity to hook students for the lesson of the day, no transition from an opening to a mini lesson to a work session... No order whatsoever! (We'll look more at rituals and routines in Chapters 10 and 11.) There were no objectives for the students to look forward to meeting when in that class, so there was chaos. Whenever Mr. Redfield would attempt to teach or require students' attention for any other reason, it would take an act of Congress that presented itself with yelling, and we saw how effective that was. Nothing was accomplished. Nothing at all.

The Experts Agree

Life is too short to have to rely on being cranky and mean to get results. An effective discipline plan will not only eliminate the need for this out-of-date strategy, but it will also allow teachers to relax and be themselves so that they can get more enjoyment out of teaching!

Discipline without Anger:
A New Style of Classroom Management, 2012
Doug Campbell (the Discipline Doctor)

Teaching students a predetermined signal for coming to attention saves time and prevents yelling, begging, and pleading at students to get their attention. The students' dignity is kept intact because they are not demeaned into coming to attention. The teacher's dignity is kept intact because the cue is delivered in a professional, caring manner.

The Classroom Management Book, 2014
Harry T. Wong & Rosemary T. Wong

When teachers react in anger instead of solving a problem, not only do they lose valuable instructional time, but they also diminish their reputations as caring, self-disciplined adults. Make it a point that you will remain calm in front of your students.

Discipline Survival Guide for the Secondary Teacher, 2011
Julia G. Thompson

Homework

Think about a time when you "yelled at a problem" or dealt harshly with solving an issue. Did it help? Keeping that problem/issue in mind, think about how you could have handled it without "yelling at it" or dealing harshly with it.

Reflect.

_____

_____

_____

_____

_____

_____

_____

_____

_____

_____

Chapter 4

Never Let 'Em See You Sweat

The most common way we give up our power is by
thinking we have none.

- **Alice Walker**

The Warm-Up / Bell Ringer

Her face was flushed. It was deep red with spots here and there of what her flesh must've looked like before she'd gotten so worked up. Flyaways from her loose ponytail were melting into the tiny beads of sweat on her forehead. The rims of her eyes were damp from the tears she'd just cried in the five minutes she'd spent in the supply closet in her classroom—the five minutes that felt like an eternity. The classroom was a mess from the fight that had broken out, and all she could do was stand in the middle of the chaos and stare at it all. Then, she cried.

Again.

And the students laughed.

Again.

In fact, they hadn't stopped laughing since the first time they'd seen her cry. Every day since that day, the Tuesday of the third week of school, they'd been finding something to do that would rile Mrs. Parbow up so much that she'd scoot herself into one of her safe spaces—the corner near her desk or the supply closet—and commune with her tears. The students had found her switch, and they flipped it every chance they got. They knew she'd cry, so they poked and prodded until they got what they wanted. And Mrs. Parbow never let them down. She cried every time.

On many occasions, I watched the students plan in the hallway before entering her class. One conversation is so vivid in my mind that it framed this chapter. May I take you to that day in the hallway?

Work Session: Ms. Ussin's Story

There were four classrooms on our hall, and as it is in most middle schools, these four classrooms were the students' core classes—math, science, social studies, and language arts—so the students could travel in a close-knit community. When it was time for class changes, the hallway was packed—our organized chaos. Students were in lines, but when all four classes were in the hallway at the same time and students were weaving through each other, it was pretty congested. On this particular day, I wanted to try to lighten the traffic, so at the first class change of the day, I decided to lead transition and have my students lined up and ready to go two minutes before the usual time. The students in the classroom directly across the hall from me would be entering my classroom at the class change, and my students would go down the hall a bit to Mrs. Parbow, instantly removing one whole class from the muddle.

As my students stood in line, naturally, they talked and talked and talked (gotta love middle schoolers). I didn't mind; they knew my expectations. As long as they were in line and not scattered abroad in the hallway, and as long as their voices couldn't be heard throughout all the earth, they were fine.

There was one group in that class that was made up of four girls and three boys. They'd become known as the crew to stir up all the ruckus in their classes. They were the masterminds behind pushing Mrs. Parbow's buttons, and that day, I learned their strategy.

I watched as they sneakily moved themselves a few inches away from their class line and formed a circle closer to the wall where they were lined up. They were close enough to the rest of the class to look like they were still in line, but far enough away that they could speak in private without their classmates hearing. I was standing at my door, seemingly preoccupied with papers they'd just submitted, but my high-beam ears were tuned in to every word they said. It was just the right distance between us for me to hear it all. By the time I fixed my focus on their conversation, they had just started talking about the exact way they would instigate an episode with Mrs. Parbow once their class got settled in the room.

Girl 1: But we can't do that cuz y'all know she gon' be by that door.

Boy 1: Yeah, she always by that door.

Girl 1: But we can sit on the other side of the class. If we sit over there, she gon' move over there cuz you know she try to be wherever we at.

They all laugh.

Girl 2: She do! She be watchin' us!

They all laugh again.

Boy 1: So who gon' do it?

Boy 2: Let me do it.

Boy 1: You can't miss, bruh. You gotta make sure it hit her.

They are bent over in laughter at Boy 1's comment.

Girl 1: And when she start crying and try to go in that closet, we gon' run and stand in front of the door.

Girl 2: But we gotta already be goin' that way when he throw the pencil cuz we not on that side of the class.

YOUR CLASSROOM OR THEIR PLAYGROUND

All: Oh, yeah!

They carry on with some indistinct talk to acknowledge their remembrance of a previous conversation.

Boy 1: So, before he throw the pencil, y'all (pointing to two of the three girls in their conversation) just get up and start walking that way.

Girl 1: Yeah, cuz she gon' be lookin' at us wondering what we doing, so her head gon' be turned and you can throw it.

They fall out laughing.

At that point, Mrs. Parbow opened her door. I didn't hear the rest of the plan, but I was sure they would go through with it. Every other day or so, there was some "major event" for Mrs. Parbow or an administrator to de-escalate in that room with that particular class. I had made it my business not to go into her classroom to get the students in order because I didn't want to undermine any of the authority she did have. I knew, too, if I went in there once, I'd have to do it every day, all year (I talk more about this in Chapter 6).

Because I knew what was in the works, I called an administrator and had him stand by Mrs. Parbow's door after I explained what I'd heard the children discuss. It was no surprise to the principal that those were the children involved. He was just about saying the names with me as I gave him the rundown. The administrator took it from there, and I went back into my classroom.

The Closing / Lesson Wrap-Up

"The Crew" was notorious for that kind of behavior in Mrs. Parbow's class. Unfortunately, her class period was their time to shine, and it was because she'd let them see her sweat. She let her guard down that one time, and they took it and ran with it like children do. It's just like when a bully sees that the prey is afraid. The bully taunts and taunts because s/he knows s/he can. S/He knows the prey will cry and cower, so s/he continues to push. S/He knows the prey won't fight back, so s/he just keeps tantalizing, and if the prey never stands up or resists the bully's treatment, the bully just keeps on. I hate that I'm even able to use this analogy for students and their teacher, but the shoe definitely fits here.

I would never tell a teacher to go into a classroom trying to be someone they're not, emulating some macho, overbearing general who is overly authoritative (because that sometimes has the same effect as having no authority at all). I would never suggest that a teacher try to be anyone but themselves as discussed in Chapter 1. I would, however, tell teachers to do what they have to do to save face.

I've wanted to cry before. I've wanted to ball up in a corner and quit. I've wanted to tell students, "I give up because y'all just aren't gettin' this," but I dared not because if I did, they would've taken over! They would instantly see my backing into a corner...my crying...my quitting as weakness, and I refused to let them—25-35 students as one unit—bully me.

Everyone loves a good show...I don't care who you are. These kids wanted a show in Mrs. Parbow's class, and pretty much every day on that "playground," a show is what they got.

And it was all because she let 'em see her sweat.

The Experts Agree

When first starting out, teachers may not naturally have much confidence. If that is the case, they need to fake it! Faking confidence and control of the classroom may be necessary even though the reality is different. Displaying confidence can help to drastically reduce behavior problems, even if it is faked. Also, if teachers pretend that they are confident and in control for a long enough period of time, they will eventually begin to believe it. A little swagger goes a long way. Acting confident and in control long enough will eventually make it true. Teachers should act quickly and decisively and never show fear.

Discipline without Anger:
A New Style of Classroom Management, **2012**
Doug Campbell (the Discipline Doctor)

From the first encounter with the teacher, students will be able to determine if the teacher is afraid of them. If there is any sign of fear in the teacher, the students will attack like a hungry lion after its prey. A fearful [urban] classroom teacher will lose respect, authority, and overall control of the classroom.

Classroom Management:
A Guide for Urban School Teachers, **2012**
Sean B. Yisrael

You must have confidence in your own ability to reach your students. If you are to be successful in overcoming the barriers to a positive discipline climate, you must communicate your belief that your students can grow and change for the better.

Discipline Survival Guide for the Secondary Teacher, **2011**
Julia G. Thompson

Homework

How do you handle being frustrated? Angry? Tired? Honestly assess yourself. These emotions will surface time and time again inside your classroom. The way you handle yourself outside of your classroom when faced with frustration, anger, and fatigue will likely be how it shows up inside your classroom. If it's not how you'd like to appear before students, put it in check now! Discover and implement new ways to cope.

Reflect with some ideas.

_____

_____

_____

_____

_____

_____

_____

_____

Chapter 5

You're Not Their Friend

Kids don't need another friend.
What they need is a parent to be a parent.

-Judge Judy

...and a teacher to be a teacher.

-Ms. Ussin

The Warm-Up / Bell Ringer

We've all had "that teacher" at least once, the teacher who wanted to be cool with students and act like a friend rather than behave like a teacher. When I was a student in middle and high school, I always felt sorry for that teacher. It was painful to watch an adult jump through teenage-sized hoops to fit into a seemingly necessary sphere of acceptance that never really even existed for them. In fact, in most cases, once those teachers cast their true selves to the side to be who they believed students wanted them to be, students lost respect for them, completely shattering whatever hope there was for the imaginary acceptance.

Know this: Regardless of what you may think or what anyone may have told you, students don't expect their teachers to even *want* to be their friends.

Let me say it again.

Students don't expect their teachers to want to be their friends.

Students expect teachers to have genuine, appropriate relationships with them. They want to feel comfortable talking to their teachers about schoolwork and academics, but they'd like to have their teachers in their circle of trusted adults too. They'd appreciate their teachers being able to guide and advise them regarding issues and concerns that arise outside of the classroom with professionalism, expertise, and wisdom. They can't get that from friends. Friends are friends, and friends do what friends do. Teachers are teachers, and teachers do what teachers do. Or at least they should.

Work Session: Ms. Ussin's Story

During the first few days of school, when teachers are introducing themselves and their expectations and walking through their syllabi and the rituals and routines for the class, students give a general, common respect for the orientation. They understand it's a new school year with a fresh start. They anticipate those first days being introductory and didactic in nature. Students know they're supposed to learn how each class will be structured for the remainder of the school year and how they're expected to behave and perform. I'd venture to say 99% of students give their undivided, most respectful attention to their teachers with honest hopes of maintaining it all year as long as their teachers consistently require it all year. (There will always be a small percentage of students, inevitably, that just color outside the lines.) Students understand, clearly, that the teacher is the authority figure, and they intend to respect the teacher as such, unless the teacher doesn't expect it. And who did I observe not expecting "the adult kind of respect" because she was more interested in being her students' friend?

Poor Ms. Eclair.

We have to visit Ms. Eclair's classroom again because on Day One of the school year, she squandered the opportunity to establish herself as the authority figure—the teacher. She was more concerned with she and her students being cronies, and it backfired. I was able to connect the dots and learn why her school years had been so difficult. It was all in how she started the year and how she presented herself to her students in the beginning. It determined how they treated her every day to the end.

Our principal, like most principals in the county, required teachers to spend the first two days of school walking through our school district's

Code of Conduct, explaining and discussing specific articles in detail. Every student was equipped with his/her own booklet so they could highlight and make notes in key places. I didn't have enough booklets for all of my students, so I decided to go next door to my neighbor's classroom to see if she had any extras. When I stepped outside of my room to make my quick dash, I saw Ms. Eclair outside of her classroom, talking to her students from the door. She said, and I quote, "I know y'all go over the Code of Conduct every year, so we're not doing that today. I don't feel like lookin' at that thang anyway. I feel like we all know the school rules, right? Don't y'all think we do? We're okay. We're good. We're not new to school. We got this."

I was floored! Teachers have autonomy and the liberty to "add themselves" into the way they do things, but even when they proceed differently, they should still do what's required, especially when it's a school-wide expectation. Every student in the school was expecting to go over the Code of Conduct on Day One because the principal had announced it as the most important item of the day. When Ms. Eclair didn't complete that task because she thought the students would prefer to hang out and chill, she set herself up for the students to disregard and disrespect her. That one act spoke more loudly to her students than her words ever would. It said:

1. Ms. Eclair doesn't follow the rules, so clearly, we can do what we want in here. If she doesn't follow mandated procedures, we don't have to follow them either—the school's or hers.
2. Ms. Eclair's not one of the real teachers. She's a teacher because it's her job, but she doesn't expect from us what other real teachers expect. (I actually heard students say this one.)
3. This class will be an easy A. She's not serious about school.

4. She's cool, kinda like on a friend level. We can run over her. And she wants to remain in our good graces, so we can take advantage of that.

There were several instances like that throughout the year where the school would be doing one thing and Ms. Eclair would be doing her own thing with her class. Often, I'd hear her in conversation with students, talking about her personal life in a way that was beyond what many teachers may insert in their lessons while teaching. And students talk. They'd tell us (other teachers) how all Ms. Eclair ever really did was talk about what was happening in her world. They said she did more talking to them than teaching, and they didn't esteem her as a teacher because of it.

And then, the backfire!

Later in the school year, after months of "befriending" her students instead of teaching and leading them, and after many parental complaints and reprimands from administration for doing so, Ms. Eclair decided to change her ways, put her foot down, and spend more time in actual instruction. The students said she was "trying to get strict." Ms. Eclair attempted to implement structure into her classes that hadn't been there all year. She began to assign insane amounts of work in class in an effort to keep students quiet. She even started issuing detentions to students for engaging in behaviors that had been acceptable all year. As you can probably imagine, the students rebelled, and understandably so. They were confused. Where had their friend gone? Why were things changing all of a sudden?

What do you mean we can't talk in class? We've been doing it all year.

What do you mean we can't walk out and go to the restroom whenever we want? We've been doing it all year.

What do you mean we have to turn in homework on time, or at all? We haven't done that all year. Come on, Ms. Eclair!

The Closing / Lesson Wrap-Up

I'll never forget meeting the teachers on my hall my first year of teaching. One of them, whom I credit as one of the most influential educators in my life, jokingly said, "We have to let them know from the beginning that we ain't playin'. That's why I don't smile until Christmas. It's strictly business until then."

Now, she, of course, wasn't saying she never smiled with her students, but what she *was* saying was her classroom was for learning and growing, not playtime. She knew if she let her students see her as loose and ingratiating in the beginning of the year, she probably wouldn't even make it to Christmas without her classroom becoming their playground.

If you start your year as the teacher-friend, you're likely to have to end it that way. It's not impossible to make a change, but doing so will be arduous. If you try to switch course and drop the hammer on your students in the middle of the year, they'll likely resent you and rebel just as Ms. Eclair's students did.

It's hard to go from friend to subordinate. Think about that person you've been working with for seven years. You have the same job description. You get paid the same. Then, he gets promoted and you have to report to him as your direct supervisor. No matter how professional you are, you both have a hard time switching from being coworkers and friends, experiencing all the same things together, to his having to enforce policy and your having to obey. You've never had to obey him before! The same is true for you and your students. Don't put yourself in the position of friend to your students and then attempt to flip it and try to be teacher and do business. In my 15 years in the classroom, on several different instructional teams, I never saw a "teacher-friend" able to make the change.

Remember this: Even the most challenging student wants a teacher who will operate with professionalism and integrity and maintain the status of key authority figure in the room. Students need boundaries like that. They want boundaries like that. Your students have enough friends. They don't need their teacher trying to be one. And guess what? You have enough friends too. You don't need your students to be your friends.

Teach them. Have fun teaching them. Teach them how to have fun learning. But keep the lines clear. They should always know you're not their friend.

The Experts Agree

While it is important that we like being with our students, a teacher's role is to be a friendly adult, not an adult friend.

Discipline Survival Guide for the
Secondary Teacher, 2011
Julia G. Thompson

While it is fine to have a goal of getting along well with students, it is dangerous to get buddy-buddy with them. When popularity is a goal, it becomes too easy to compromise fairness and professionalism to try to reach it. Also, students will usually recognize when a teacher is concerned with being popular and manipulate them.

Discipline without Anger:
A New Style of Classroom Management, 2012
Doug Campbell (the Discipline Doctor)

Forgetting that you are a role model can lead to a loss of respect. Students have a fairly clear idea of the behaviors they want from the adults in their lives. Make a point of being the adult you would want your students to grow into.

Discipline Survival Guide for the
Secondary Teacher, 2011
Julia G. Thompson

Homework

Do you remember any of your teachers who were "teacher-friends"? How were they perceived by their students? What are some specific things you remember the teacher(s) saying and/or doing that qualified them to be "teacher-friends"? Did students treat that teacher(s) like other teachers?

Reflect.

Chapter 6

Don't You Dare Call Mr. Gordon!

Give a man a fish and you feed him for a day.
Teach a man to fish and you feed him for a lifetime.

-Chinese Proverb

The Warm-Up / Bell Ringer

My students were returning to my class from P.E. As usual, they were rowdy and totally amped from their hour of nonstop physical activity. Adrenaline was always high with that 2nd period class. But this day was different.

Their normal buzz had an unusual tone. It was tense. It was aggressive and cross. The laughs, jokes, and playful jostling that I was accustomed to witnessing as they rounded the corner and took the 20 or so steps to my end-of-the-hall classroom was replaced with expletives, threats, and glares that would kill if they could. They didn't walk in the award-winning straight line they'd become known for throughout the school. Instead, they were scattered about in various clusters of those who were involved in what had caused the severance and those who were attempting to steer clear of it.

By the time they approached my door, trickling into the classroom one by one, daring each other to get too close, they kept the boiling fuss somewhat contained because they respected me and the environment they'd come to know as peaceful. It wasn't too long, though, before what was happening in the hallway piped up right there in my classroom.

Work Session: Ms. Ussin's Story

They didn't want to upset me. I could see it in the way their chests puffed up with air as they tried to hold back their words. One young man, whose nose I swore was releasing dragon-like smoke, stared out the window near his desk and just repeatedly tapped his ink pen on the desk. I knew it was his way of managing the anger. It was all he knew to do not to blow the roof.

I didn't say anything. I could read the room. I knew anything I said in that atmosphere would go in one ear and out the other. They were too angry with one another to pay me any real attention. The class, as a whole, was still somewhat subdued, but the vexed buzz, which manifested through infuriated mumbles and groans, never stopped with about six of the boys in the class, the ones who'd played in the basketball game that had them up in arms at P.E. I later learned that one of the boys had cheated and sparked the blaze that set the fire in motion. The boys from the opposing team wanted to hurt him and make him pay.

And then it happened.

"Bruh, I'm tellin' you. You keep lookin' over here at me like you wan' do su'um, and we gon' have to do su'um."

Out of nowhere. Just like that. From hushed mumbles to a blatant, public dare. And there was no backing down from that dare. Nope. Not with ego in play.

The shouting match was on.

When the commotion hadn't ceased after a full minute, Mr. Gordon, my next-door neighbor and teammate, stepped into my classroom and told the boys to squash whatever it was they'd been arguing about. He went on about how the rest of the students were sitting in their seats waiting on me to start class, but because they were being belligerent, everyone else's education was being put on hold.

"Get yourselves settled so class can begin! And do it NOW!" he barked.

The boys still took a moment to release steam, but they eventually came to themselves, settled in their seats, and focused their attention on me.

Mr. Gordon was protective of me because it was my first year teaching. Although there hadn't been very many problems in my room, he would still peek his head in every now and then. He'd established himself as someone I could go to with questions too. He wanted to make sure I was okay.

After Mr. Gordon's intervention, things were going well, but at some point toward the end of class, one of the boys said something that stirred the pot all over again. In the middle of all the hype, one student said, "Y'all stop before she call Mr. Gordon over here."

I froze.

To them, it appeared that I had called Mr. Gordon over to my room at the top of class. In their eyes, I needed Mr. Gordon to bring order to my room. To them, Mr. Gordon was the law. And I didn't like that. I didn't like it at all.

The Closing / Lesson Wrap-Up

Now, don't get me wrong. I knew I could call on Mr. Gordon if I needed him, and I wasn't so high and mighty that I felt I didn't need him. That wasn't it at all. I was new to teaching; I knew that full well. And even more than that, the school session had begun in early August; I didn't get hired to teach until November. There was a lot that could work against me with that alone. I needed Mr. Gordon and the rest of my team in my corner.

Our students had already come to know Mr. Gordon as the teacher who didn't play. The children barely ever uttered a word in his class. He had order—militant structure—in his room, but I didn't want them thinking the authority that was next door in Mr. Gordon's room was the same rule in my room. There had to be an established order in my room, so when our students were in my room, they would know I was the law.

From that one episode, I could clearly see that it would be to my detriment if I ever made it a habit to call on someone else to "put out my fires." If my students saw that I couldn't handle their behaviors and that I always had to call someone else in to chastise them, they'd never respect me as the authority figure. I'd never be able to set order in the room because they wouldn't expect me to enforce it. If they went outside of any of the parameters I'd set, they wouldn't expect consequences from me because I wouldn't know how to uphold them. They had to see me as the deputy—the one who issued "sentences" when they broke the law in my class. This is why, years later, I never attempted to control what was going on in Mrs. Parbow's class (Chapter 4) or any other teacher's class. They had to be the sheriffs in their own towns.

From that day forward, I refused to call Mr. Gordon to my classroom for behavior issues. Whatever came up, I dealt with it, and I believe that's what every teacher should do, especially in those first couple of years. (Violent, life-threatening behavior issues are a different case.) This is when you're learning who you are as a teacher and discovering what you'll allow as acceptable in your classroom. This is when you learn what works with the children you're teaching and what doesn't. The last thing you need is someone stepping in doing everything for you, seizing your power, undermining your authority, and snatching your ability to establish your own way.

So... whatever you do...

Don't you dare call Mr. Gordon!

The Experts Agree

The teacher is not a buddy or a chum, but neither is the teacher a warden or a tyrant. The teacher is the professional responsible for keeping the class focused on what is being taught, for maintaining discipline in a fair and consistent manner, and for ensuring the alignment and reliability and validity of evaluation. The teacher must retain the right of ultimate authority in the interest of the safety and physical, emotional and personal, and intellectual well-being of the students.

Instruction: A Models Approach, 2007
Mary Alice Gunter,
Thomas H. Estes, &
Susan L. Mintz

Homework

One of my former pastors once said in a sermon, "Anything with two heads is a monster." It's true! There's only one teacher assigned to your classroom, and that one teacher is the authority figure and final say in the room. What do you know you need to work on now to ensure you're able to put out your own fires as the authority figure in your classroom?

_____

_____

_____

_____

_____

_____

_____

_____

_____

_____

_____

Chapter 7

Why Aren't You Ready?

If you fail to plan, you plan to fail.

-Benjamin Franklin

The Warm-Up / Bell Ringer

Have you ever called a restaurant for takeout and the person who took your call said your food would be ready in 15-20 minutes? If you're like me, when someone says your food will be ready in 15 minutes, you don't show up until 25 minutes later. If they say it'll be ready in 20 minutes, you don't show up until 30 minutes later. I like to give the 10-minute benefit of the doubt, or what I call "mishap time" because there's nothing worse than calling in for takeout and it not being ready to take out. I expect the food to be hot and ready when I get there.

And students are the same way.

Students expect their teachers to have the classroom and the plan for the day hot and ready when they show up. No matter who the child is, he wants things all set when he gets to your class. And she can be the one who religiously misbehaves in your class, but even she wants you and the classroom primed for learning when she gets there.

Children know school is a place that operates systematically, so they anticipate everything to be orderly. They know from the moment they arrive at school in the morning to the time they depart, there will be set policies and procedures in place for them to follow. Take the school where I ended my stint as a classroom teacher, for example. A normal school day is strategically structured from student arrival to dismissal.

Every morning, buses haul students from their neighborhoods to the school cafeteria. Students exit their buses and enter the cafeteria through the only open door. Once in, students do one of two things: (1) If they want breakfast, they walk through the serving line and then take their breakfast to the right side of the cafeteria where students sit only if they're actually eating. (2) If they don't want breakfast, they walk to the left side of the cafeteria where there is no eating, and they have a seat.

If students walk to school or if they're car riders, they are expected to walk to the cafeteria, enter through the only open door, and follow one of the two aforementioned procedures. No other doors at the school are open for student entry during the "before school" hours. Students are allowed in the cafeteria only under the supervision of the Connections/Specials teachers, at least one administrator, and sometimes, the school safety officer.

When the breakfast portion of the day has concluded and the bell rings for students to head to their homeroom classes, the Connections/Specials teachers dismiss students in an orderly fashion, by tables, clearing one side of the cafeteria at a time. As students navigate through the halls, teachers and other faculty and staff are on duty at every turn, especially at the busy intersections and high-traffic areas, ensuring students' uneventful arrival to their classrooms where their teachers stand at the doors to greet them. Students know this routine, and they know staff will be in place to monitor them.

Once students are in class, they complete a bell-ringer activity or morning work while waiting on the academic portion of the day to commence. Then, the tardy bell rings, which is the signal for students to wrap up their morning work and prepare to give attention to the morning announcements. The morning announcements begin with the Pledge of Allegiance and a moment of silence. Students know to stand for the pledge and wait until they're told to be seated to listen to the announcements. After announcements, students follow their grade-level schedules for their five classes. The 6th, 7th, and 8th grade halls are on different schedules, going to Connections classes and lunch at strictly appointed times.

When at lunch, each class, under its teacher's direction, walks in line to one of the serving lanes to get a meal. Then, as is the requirement, students file into their class's lunch table without skipping any seats. They raise their hands to get an adult's attention if they need anything because they aren't allowed to walk around the lunch room for any reason at all. When the lunch period has ended, teachers, one at a time, dismiss their classes to dispose of their trash. The classes line up and report back to their classrooms.

At the close of the school day, when the bell sounds to signal the end of the academic period, the afternoon announcements begin. The announcer dismisses walkers and car riders by grade. Then, the announcer calls bus numbers, and as students hear their buses being called, they exit their classrooms and head to the bus loading zone to board them.

Students *expect* this type of order at school. They expect for teachers and staff, regular rituals and routines, materials, and whatever else is necessary for their academic success to be all systems go from the beginning to the end of the day. And in the place where they spend most of their school day—the classroom—that expectation is the greatest because for what other reason do schools even exist?

The Work Session: Ms. Ussin's Story

When Mrs. Roma dragged herself into the school building every day, there was no doubt that she'd rather be elsewhere. The toddler-like pout in her lips, her overly obvious, sad eyes, her heavy, slumped shoulders, and the below-speed-limit pace—dead giveaways.

Every day, without fail, she would stroll in, just as the tardy bell was ringing, usually ignoring her co-workers' warm "Good Morning" greetings, or barely responding to them with a nod. When she would finally make it to her classroom, where most of her students had grown accustomed to sitting along the wall outside the room, waiting, and where her teammates had become weary of daily keeping watch, she'd take her time shifting her purse from one shoulder to the other to free up her dominant hand so she could slowly unlock the door. Without acknowledging any students, she'd mope in while students passed her by to get to their seats, walk to her desk, sit in her chair right in front of the computer that was connected to the Promethean board, and listlessly power everything up.

Make note that Mrs. Roma's students were missing the homeroom period where they should have been doing morning work or some thought-provoking task to activate their brains for the day. Instead, again, most students were seated along the wall outside of her classroom being monitored by the other teachers on the hall as they stood at their doors to receive their students.

And where were Mrs. Roma's other students who weren't on the wall? What were they doing?

That handful of students was wandering the halls, ducking off into restrooms and other lightly monitored spaces, getting into mischief and causing problems. They'd learned Mrs. Roma's schedule and knew she wouldn't be on time. They knew when she got there, she wouldn't be standing at her door because she would be getting herself situated at " her desk, finding her way for the day. They had the perfect, wide-open opportunity to do what their hearts desired (if they didn't get caught, and some days they didn't). They could walk into the classroom right along with Mrs. Roma and the rest of the students at the tardy bell, and they did. It's no surprise that so many issues started in and around her classroom. When students have idle time, it's bound to happen. Uuuuugh! My heart breaks every time I even think of this scenario!

Every teacher has rough mornings from time to time. There may be a few days in the school year when you'll be late. But everyday lateness being the norm? That's so unfair to the students! Teachers are required to sign in before the school day starts because that time of preparation is necessary. Most teachers arrive well before the designated sign-in time because they know the importance of readiness. They know how vital it is to receive students and welcome them in. They understand the significance of students entering a classroom, seeing the plan for the day hot and ready to go for them. And this should be you. Don't let your lack of readiness and preparedness strip your students of the order and consistency they crave in the entirety of their school day.

The Closing / Lesson Wrap-Up

How can you show up to class *with* your students and be ready for them?

I've gotten to school late a good few times in my career and ended up getting to my classroom after my students, or arriving at the same time as them. I can assure you, no matter what I may have had prepared from the day before, I wasn't ready when I walked in that door. If nothing else, I was out of sorts simply because I'd just gotten there. Who wouldn't need a few minutes to at least just get their bearings straight?

No matter how much my students respected me and knew my expectations of them... no matter how understanding they may have been in knowing that late days sometimes happen, I was still the cause of their not having the consistency, readiness, and preparation they expected from their teacher. They were inadvertently forced into idle, unstructured time, time when they could've gotten into mischief, and time that allowed their brains to shift from focusing on the reason they were there.

I've said it once, but it's worth mentioning again here: Children want order. They want rules, boundaries, and guidelines. They thrive when they follow set rituals and routines. They want expectations set for them, even if they act like they don't, but they want the one who sets the guidelines to require that they be met. When even one thing is out of place, or the schedule deviates from the norm, it shatters the consistency they require.

Why aren't you ready?

- Why didn't you test that website before you started the lesson?
- Why didn't you make the copies when you were on that side of the building? The machine's not out of service anymore!
- Why didn't you calculate those scores yesterday so you'd know what particular stations students need in the rotation today?

When you're not ready, it affects your students. Period. Let school be the place (the only place for some) where they have order at every point in their day. And if it's not every point in their day, don't let the period in the day where they don't have structure be your class.

Ask Mrs. Roma. She'll tell you that her homeroom class was a playground. Or maybe she won't tell you, but anyone who worked with her will.

Why, oh, why wasn't she ready?

The Experts Agree

Every decision we make as teachers is one that has the potential to affect the discipline climate in our classrooms in a negative or positive way. Making the commitment to be fully prepared for class every day is a sensible choice with the potential for significantly positive results.

Discipline Survival Guide for the
Secondary Teacher, **2011**
Julia G. Thompson

An organized and prepared leader is a healthy leader. The more investment you place in preparation, the more you accomplish. Preparation is essential in organizing your day.

If You Don't Feed the Teachers, They Eat the Students!
Guide to Success for Administrators and Teachers, **2010**
Dr. Neila A. Connors

Being prepared is essential—no matter the endeavor. The effective teacher plans, and then plans some more. Plan for every situation that could arise. Don't think second by second about what needs to be done. Have a plan. Follow the plan, and you'll be surprised how successful you can be.

The Classroom Management Book, **2014**
Harry T. Wong & Rosemary T. Wong

Homework

Reflect on a time when someone was supposed to be prepared for you but wasn't. What happened? How did the lack of preparation make you feel? Reflect on a time when you weren't prepared for someone when you should have been. How did it make them feel?

Planning Period

It was October in my 12th school year, and I had a long, self-care weekend getaway planned with two of my dearest friends. I was scheduled to fly out on Thursday night to meet up with them. By the end of the workday on that Tuesday, my classroom was already in order, and lesson plans were scripted to perfection for our very capable 6th grade "team choice" substitute to take over on Friday. Talk about excited! Imagine how deflated I was when the trip got cancelled because one of my friends fell ill. I was devastated, to say the least. After the initial shock, and a couple hours alone to regroup, I resolved that nothing would keep me from "self-caring" that weekend. Since I already had a substitute in place, I took the Friday off to relax and run errands.

En route from my last errand to my relax-a-thon at home, I was thinking about all the things I wanted to do that weekend. I was planning to write a couple of chapters in this book. I was planning to deep clean both bathrooms in my house. I was ready to kick back and watch a movie. Maybe two. But I was jarred from those thoughts when I realized I'd be passing the school where I had taught for four years before transferring to the school where I was currently teaching. I said to myself, *"I can stop in and visit some of my colleagues!"* I'd built so many good relationships there that I didn't have to think twice. Once the thought entered my mind, it was a done deal. When I approached the school, I turned into the teacher lot, parked my car, and headed to the front office to sign in.

Just as I said I would, I made surprise visits to my former coworkers' classrooms, staying in each room 10 or 15 minutes to watch them in action. Naturally, I became more interested in the children because the teacher in me just couldn't help it. I walked from desk to desk and from table to table to see what the children were doing. I had them talk me through their assignments so I could gauge their understanding. I wanted to know if they were just doing work or if they were learning. In some classes, students were just doing work. In other classes, students were learning.

The same was true for behavior. There were some classes where all students were on task. Everyone was engaged either in instruction or in an active work session where the teacher was merely a facilitator of students owning their learning. In other classes, there was no instruction at the time of my visit, and there was no active work session, but there *was* a lot of chaos. Students were all about the room, in conversations amongst themselves. In one class, a teacher was so engulfed in what he was doing on his computer at his desk that he didn't even notice I'd entered the room. There was no way he could've known what the students had been doing for God knows how long before I appeared.

I ended my visit in the cafeteria eating lunch with one of my former teammates-turned-good friend. We had the opportunity to talk about old times and share a little about what was happening in our classrooms that year. My friend introduced me to her new teammate, who was a first-year teacher. The first-year teacher and I began to talk, and she asked where I was teaching. When I told her the school, her eyes lit up. She said she'd attended that school and had so much respect for it not just because she'd gone there, but because of its magnet status and how much positive academic attention it brought to the city of Augusta. After we got past that, she followed up with a question that I will never forget. That question plagued my mind all weekend. That question was a very loud reminder of why I was writing this book. It sent me right home to my book notes so I could quickly encapsulate everything I'd shared in my response to her. The question had caught me off guard in the sense that I didn't think our conversation was headed that way, but it was unexpectedly right on time. I'd been answering it within myself and wanting to have some real discourse about it for a while. It's a question that I hope this book addresses well and that I hope will shape the remainder of your time as a classroom teacher. She said, "Do you think there's a difference in student behaviors at different schools?"

I knew what she was really asking. You see, teachers in our district would look at teachers like me who taught at one of our four magnet schools, and think (and some would just straight up say), "Oh, you don't have to deal with what we have to deal with. All of your students are angels." I've taught at a magnet school and I've taught at traditional middle schools, so I've seen it all, and nothing could be further from the truth. Please allow me to frame this answer before I share my response to her.

I remember walking into my principal's office at Tubman Middle School on that November day in 2006. It would be my first day as a classroom teacher. Tubman happened to be the lowest performing, needs-improvement middle school in the county at the time, and the student behavior matched the academic performance. Gang activity was present. Fights were commonplace. Loud hallways were the norm. But the majority of the student body wanted to learn. There were, as in most places, some knuckleheads who tried to completely disrupt the learning environment, but for the most part, I remember teaching those children how to climb through the sky and sit on the moon! They learned as much as they did in my class that year because they were hungry for it. I wouldn't know for months that they were that eager to learn, but once I saw their hunger, I never stopped feeding it.

That first day in my principal's office, I really had no clue what I was getting into. I had some idea, but nothing could have prepared me for the moment those students were completely released into my control. The principal said to me, "If you can teach here, you can teach anywhere." He didn't lie. That first year of teaching set me up to become the educator I am, with the ability to step into any environment and cause learning to take place.

The school year had begun in early August, so the students on that team had had four "permanent" substitutes. They had seen so much change and were so tired of being tossed around and grouped into other classes that their hope was almost gone. For the first couple of weeks of my being there, there was a "ho hum" across all four of my classes that screamed, "Let's just endure her for a couple weeks because soon she'll be gone too." I could see it. I could hear it. And because it was so clear in my eyes and in my ears, I could just about smell it. I had to remind them on many occasions, for quite some time, that I wasn't going anywhere. I couldn't leave them. They'd been through enough.

I remember one sweet little boy, whom I'm still in contact with today. He's a married man serving in the Army, and I still see him as my little angel. That first day, when I stepped foot in my classroom, calling roll and passing out assignments, reviewing expectations, going over everything in great detail making sure they understood, he just sat in his seat, kicked his little feet that barely touched the floor, and softly clapped his hands to himself. His gestures that expressed his excitement made me look in his direction, and I'll never forget what came out of his mouth in that moment. He said, "Oh my God! She's so organized! Yes! Finally!" He smiled the entire class period. His eyes followed me everywhere I walked around the room. He raised his hand to answer any question I asked, and if I needed a child to do anything, he, of course, volunteered his services. Charles is learning, for the first time, in this book, that he, second only to the call that I believe God has on my life, is the reason I didn't leave them too. There were days I wanted to leave, believe me, but his outward expression of gratefulness, I knew, was shared by the majority of the rest of my students inwardly.

Later, I'd learn through gifts and other tokens of appreciation that they had never had a Language Arts teacher like me, and they were the reason I had to continue creating environments for children to be able to learn and excel, even if our environment was nestled inside a larger, chaotic one.

When I left Tubman after four years of teaching 8th grade, I went to one of the magnet schools to teach 7th grade. At the magnet school, I saw some of the same types of students. Because students came from their zoned public schools from all over the county to attend the magnet school, there was a bit of a melting pot sitting in all of my classes the four years I spent at the magnet school. I had students who were hungry to learn, and I had students who weren't. I had students who cared about their grades, and students who didn't. I had students who knew how to behave and others who found ways to misbehave. It was the same way at my first school. The one thing that was different at the magnet school, though, was the school's climate.

Children knew when they attended the magnet school, they were attending a school of excellence. They knew there was an expectation. They knew foolishness wasn't tolerated and that if they slipped academically and/or behaviorally, there would be consequences. The environment was one that was conducive for learning, and every member of the faculty and staff protected that environment. We reminded students, often, that they were magnet school students and should behave and perform as such. They were reminded that behaviors that may be accepted in other places weren't accepted there. My first year at the magnet school, in the first few weeks of the first quarter, I witnessed a handful of my students think they'd be able to continue behaving the way they had before. I could see some of them wanting to misbehave and even wanting to pull others along with them, but then I'd see that the others wouldn't play along because they'd already gained a clear understanding of what happens in that magnet school environment. The wannabes stuck out like sore thumbs and had to adapt to the culture and climate of the school because there was an expectation. Those who adapted stayed and flourished. Those who didn't were either dismissed from the school for one reason or another, or eventually chose to leave.

So, with all of that having been said, let's go back to the question from the first-year teacher. She asked, "Do you think there's a difference in student behaviors at different schools?"

I told her, "I don't think student behaviors are different, as a whole. I think environments dictate student behavior. When I taught here (the school I was visiting that day), I had the occasional student who would show out and try to put on for their classmates because they'd seen it done a time or two in the hallway or in other classes, but when I explained to them, and showed them, daily, what happens in *my* classroom, that foolishness of theirs was shut down. At this school, behaviors are allowed. There's not enough consistency from classroom to classroom and across the administrative staff, so students are allowed to do what they do. At my school (the magnet school), there are students sitting in my classroom who would act just like the students act here if they were allowed to. Honey, some of them are just waiting on an opportunity to let loose, but because the environment doesn't condone it, they adapt to the environment's expectation."

As we venture on into the next section of the book and look at what you should do in your classroom, remember that you can't always control the climate of the school, but you can always control the temperature in your own classroom. You control the thermostat, so the temperature is whatever you say it's going to be. It can be your classroom, or it can be their playground. You choose.

Section 2

Final Exam

Chapter 8

Be You

You change the world by being yourself.

-Yoko Ono

The Warm-Up / Bell Ringer

In this chapter, you may see a repeat here and there of some of the ideas presented in Chapter 1 (Are You Being You?) Naturally, after asking if you're being you, there *has* to be a follow-up on *how* to be you, so stick with me. This chapter helps it all connect, and to set the foundation for that smooth connection, I need to restate the overarching thought from Chapter 1: *Students can sniff out a phony a mile away.* It's true. Children are the best "people readers." They know if their teachers are being themselves.

Unfortunately, one major mistake many teachers make (especially first-year teachers) is assuming they have to perform magic tricks and jump through hoops to engage their students in the learning process. That assumption is a far cry from the truth. All any teacher really needs is to care about children, master the content they're expected to teach, and be themselves.

The Work Session: Ms. Ussin's Story

I'm a storyteller; it's one of my God-given gifts and one I've come to appreciate as a highly effective tool for teaching life lessons. I write stories in my journal some mornings when I'm having prayer and quiet time. I write stories in the Notes app on my phone when I have to sit and wait in my car for an extended period of time or at my gate in the airport. Those stories usually surface in conversations with mentees or in a talk I deliver on stage. Shucks! I sometimes spout stories in the moment when I'm standing before an audience. (Those are the best!) Even my first published book is a compilation of stories called—get this—*Stories That Teach Girls: A 30-Day Walk Through Girls' Life Lessons with God's Word.* Stories just ooze from my pores. I could probably write them in my sleep.

So, since storytelling is such a solid strand in my DNA, obviously, I use it quite a bit to teach my students. And why wouldn't I? If I teach with stories in every other area of my life, why not use them to teach in my classroom, the place I always considered my main stage? Why would I not bring "me" into the classroom, where I spend the bulk of my days with the little people who matter so much to me? That would be crazy, right? Yeah. I agree. It would be crazy. Many teachers are doing it, though—using their natural giftings in every space and place but their classrooms. I even found myself doing it one year.

In all my years as a teacher, I never struggled to connect with my students until the 2020-2021 school year—the COVID year. Building instant and lasting relationships with my students and developing community in each of my classes would usually happen effortlessly, so the first few months of that school year when it didn't happen, I have to say right out, it was tough. I couldn't understand how I had an immediate connection with only one of my four classes, somewhat of a gel with another, and absolutely no bond with the other two. Devastatingly heartbreaking. It made teaching difficult. I was exhausted every day from working well beyond my normal efforts to reach students who were only in my class every day because it was listed on their schedules.

Were they respectful? Sure. I had still established order in my room and made my expectations known. My students understood my classroom wouldn't be a playground. Regardless of our connecting instinctively or not, that one thing was clear.

Were they attentive? Yes, they were, but that was only because they were respectful. They gave me their attention because they honored my position as teacher, not because they had bought into me. They had no genuine interest in my class or anything I was teaching. This was my most hurtful realization.

Were they learning? No. They were completing assignments because they cared about their grades. They were doing the work because they knew that's what was required of them, but I knew they were only grasping concepts on a surface level. As Dwayne Reed, one of the amazing educators I follow on Instagram, said (and I paraphrase), I had nothing but robots because I had no relationship.

Spoiler Alert: Things did get better, but not until I finally discerned that I'd been holding back. I hadn't been myself, the Ms. Ussin who tells stories to enliven everything she teaches. The Ms. Ussin who sings and dances up and down "the catwalk" in her classroom. The Ms. Ussin who gets all up in her students' business to know who they are, what they like, and how she can better teach them. I had been a robot too…a machine, welcoming students into the classroom, following the curriculum map and teaching the lessons, and assessing the students' work. Nothing more, nothing less. I was the teacher in one corner of the room, standing back and watching my students in the other corner. There was a wall dividing us, and we all desperately needed that wall to come down.

It hit me one day in November, after having been in school since early September, that in a sense, I'd allowed everything going on with COVID to ground me. The CDC, our district leaders, and our school administrators were stressing the importance of being fully masked at all times, washing and sanitizing our hands as often as possible, wiping down every high-traffic area that likely received human touch, and maintaining distance from our co-workers and students. We ate breakfast and lunch in our classrooms, every person at their individual, socially distanced desk. We walked the halls like soldiers, right side of the hallway northbound and left side southbound, from destination to destination, an unusual hush hovering with every transition throughout the building.

The first few weeks of school, I was tense. I was nervous about getting too close to a child's desk or having any child meet me at mine. I didn't even want to give a student a "good job" pat on the shoulder for fear of them feeling I'd done something "wrong" or being called out by co-workers or administrators for disregarding COVID safety protocol. It was a whole new "school world," like nothing we'd ever seen, and I honestly wasn't comfortable navigating in it. I didn't know how to engage without being in my students' personal space as I was accustomed to, so I locked up and froze. It seemed better to be aloof, physically and relationally, because disaster could strike with one or many of us contracting COVID and the school having to shut down. (We had two school shutdowns and a few grade-level shutdowns.) I went to school every day with the discomfort of those uncertainties swarming in my heart and mind, causing me to completely disengage, and it greatly affected the dynamics of my relationships with my students.

After seeing my teammates being themselves with our students, even while observing COVID precautions, and seeing our students respond to and engage with them, I knew I had to shake myself out of that stupor and find a way to get back to Ms. Ussin. She'd been "away" long enough! My students needed me to be me—all of me—so they could connect and really learn from me, so I pushed through and loosened up and found my "Ms. Ussin groove."

I started telling my stories as I taught, incorporating them in just about every lesson. As was the case with classes in previous years, it wasn't long before students began to ask for more stories.

Singing and dancing around the room became the norm for me, as it had been all my years with every other class. Dance is my first love. How can it not be a part of my instruction? It wasn't long before the familiar singalongs and dance breaks were happening in my room. My students didn't dread entering my room anymore. They were no longer just respectfully sitting through lessons and activities. They were excitedly engaged, and it was because I was myself—all of me. Every bit of Ms. Ussin. And with her, they were finally able to connect.

The Closing / Lesson Wrap-Up

You're a gifted musician who also loves teaching Math. Your students know you as the numbers guy, but they are clueless when it comes to your music? Why? How could music live in you and not become a part of your instruction in some way?

Your undergraduate degree is in Fine Arts with a minor in English. Before you decided to teach English, you made a living with your visual art—sketching, drawing, sculpting, and painting. How is it that your students aren't learning to use art to illustrate their stories and to "color" their writing? They don't even know you can draw because it's never shown up in any of your instruction. How stifling is it to go to work every day, all day and never tap into the creative outlet that powers you and gives you peace? Why not bring that peace to your classroom and teach your students how to live in that tranquility with you? I'm sure they'd love to see who you are, the whole you, outside of just the teacher who enhances their reading and writing skills.

Every one of your skills…all of who you are should be infused in your instruction throughout the school year. Your students need you to be you.

The Experts Agree

It takes energy to be different from whom you really are. The more you have to maintain the illusion of difference, the more drained you will end up. By contrast, if you behave as yourself, you don't have to spend as much energy.

The Real Me: Find and Express Your Authentic Self, 2017
Mark Eyre

Humanness is so essential in dealing with the business of education and its many challenges.

If You Don't Feed the Teachers, They Eat the Students!
Guide to Success for Administrators and Teachers, 2010
Dr. Neila A. Connors

Homework

You're more creative than you think.
Use what you've been given.
Teachers definitely beg, borrow, and steal,
But there's nothing more powerful than YOU, the real
deal.

–Ms. Ussin

What are some of your gifts/talents? What are some skills that come naturally for you that you enjoy? Take a moment to think through how those things can be used in your classroom to make your lessons engaging for your students. Write them below.

_____

_____

_____

_____

_____

_____

_____

_____

Chapter 9

Build Relationships

No significant learning can occur without a significant relationship.

- James Comer

The Warm-Up / Bell Ringer

Theodore Roosevelt said, "Nobody cares how much you know until they know how much you care." No truer words have ever been spoken, words that are true in every walk of life. Take your family life, for instance.

Would you invite just anyone into your home to babysit your children while you're away for a long weekend? I'm sure you wouldn't. A woman from the babysitting service could have credentials and shining reviews a mile long. She could know all there is to know about loving and caring for children, and you may even applaud that, but you don't *know* her, and she doesn't *know* your children. Clearly, she won't care enough about your children to nurture them the way you would.

Your children are too precious to leave in just anyone's hands. You won't entrust them in a stranger's care or with someone who doesn't have a familiar, loving connection with them. Relationship is what would make the difference when considering a caregiver. And it's relationship that will make the difference in your students deciding if they will "receive care" from you.

Children understand that they're in school to learn. When they enter your classroom, they believe you to be the chief source of knowledge that will teach them what they need to know and prepare them for progression to the next level. Students generally respect their teachers for that alone; they want to learn from their teachers. The question is, *how* will your students learn from you?

Will they put forth their absolute best effort in your class, or will they do just enough to be able to say they did what was expected of them? In the April 2019 Waterford.org article, *Why Strong Teacher Relationships Lead to Student Engagement and a Better School Environment*, contributing author, F.S. Reis da Luz, said, "Positive connections with your students can raise their intrinsic motivation to learn." Students who have meaningful relationships with their teachers tend to give their all with those teachers, even on difficult tasks and assignments that they'd likely forego.

Will they be self-starters in your class, engaging in regular, independent explorative learning, or will they do only what you ask or assign? Students who have positive relationships with their teachers desire to please those teachers, so they often display an ability to take initiative and the responsibility for their own learning. They self-regulate, "step up to the plate," and go the extra mile.

Will they be excited about your class, even if they're not fans of the subject or content you teach, or will they dread your class, even though you teach content they love? Children who don't like what you teach could still love your class because they love you, and they could potentially perform better than they ever have in the subject(s) they despise most.

Relationships are everything! They can make or break an entire classroom operation. This is why you must spend time building relationships with every one of your students.

At one of the schools where I taught for four years, my understanding of the need for positive teacher-student relationships intensified tremendously from my first to my last year there. That school wasn't the lowest performing middle school in our district, but it wasn't the highest either. We didn't have the worst behavior problems that were reported from middle schools in the county, but our school was certainly not on any list for setting behavioral standards for others to follow. We had our share of problems, and to be quite frank, the kids could be hard to teach.

The children knew their school had a reputation for being "bad," and because they'd heard it so much, that seed was planted in their minds. They had adapted to what they'd been called. (More of that in the BONUS Chapter.) The entire student body, of course, didn't adopt that line of thinking. There was certainly an oasis inside of the school. Many students chose to defy the stereotypes and become known in the county as academic giants, athletic powerhouses, and prodigious talents. So much positivity poured out of those school walls, but an undeniable stench filled the air because of blatant misbehavior. When those overt, unruly behaviors entered my classroom, because they definitely did, they didn't last long. I tuned into those children who acted out, and I began to "research" them. I studied them. I learned their patterns. I discovered what they liked and didn't like. I determined what worked for them and what didn't, and I used that to build relationships with them, which caused them to trust me and strive to be their best for me. Over the years, I witnessed some of those students misbehave with every other teacher on the team yet enter my classroom as model students and perform as such, every day. It was all because of the relationships I formed with those students. Once I saw how this worked, I made it my business to form a unique connection with every student. Difficult? Yes! But not impossible, and immensely rewarding. My third year at the school is where I saw this play out best.

The Work Session: Ms. Ussin's Story

My principal had some freedom to incorporate new exploratory classes into the school schedule, and with our demographic, she knew some type of dance and/or expression class would be a hit. Because I had formed a special dance group with some of the girls at the school my first year there, the administrative staff presented me with an offer to teach a dance class as a part of the regular school schedule through the

Connections/Exploratory track. As you've already read, dance is my first love. It's my getaway. It's the one thing I love just as much as teaching Lang. Arts. I was grateful for the opportunity to get away from the same ole' routine I'd been in for eight years at that point. Exciting and refreshing, but terribly nerve-wracking at the same time.

This class wouldn't be the typical dance class where students willingly enrolled because they were interested. I wouldn't be met with skilled dancers who'd already acquired core movement vocabulary or even possessed basic rhythm. This class was going to be like every other exploratory class—students would be scheduled in based on numbers. I would see 80% of the student body in my class by the end of the school year. Not only would I have to face the "One Size Fits All" scheduling, but I'd have to share space (the gym) with P.E. classes. The dance class was housed in one of the gym classrooms and had to convert from a traditional learning space for theoretical and historical instruction to a dance space that was big enough to accommodate only six or seven dancers, comfortably, if we were dancing full-out modern choreographed pieces. Some days, it worked like magic, but most days it was disastrous. I would have to regularly consult with the P.E. coach to schedule days and times for the dance class to have the entire gym floor and days for us to "go half court." On half-court days, we couldn't compete with basketballs and volleyballs flying everywhere. Our music was usually snuffed out by the loud, boisterous non-stop action. The boys in my class, as you can imagine, tuned out the moment we stepped foot onto our half of the gym floor and saw 3-on-3 in full swing on the other half, and the girls, most of them, were too embarrassed to participate because of all the eyes from the other side of the gym being on them.

I worked so hard in those first months to just establish the purpose of the class that it almost drained me of my love for it, but out of respect for me and my love for dance (although that love almost seemed to be slowly fading away), the students did what I expected of them. That kept me afloat. When they were required to watch videos they hated and learn boring dance history while the gym was fully charged and piping outside our door, they did it. When the gym floor was no longer an option and we had to contrive our own dance space, daily moving tables and stacking chairs in our matchbox classroom to accommodate 18-22 dancing bodies, they did it. But only a few enjoyed it. Only a handful, who were just naturally interested in the class, actually took pride in what they were learning and doing. Because I was swimming so hard upstream to simply maintain, I had forgotten to view my students as people. I hadn't taken the time to intentionally build any relationships. As a result, both my students and I were dying. We were all just showing up to class because our schedules said we should. And some weren't even doing that.

The light came on for me one day when I granted my students free play in the gym after they'd taken a test. One of my female 8th grade students, whom I'd taught Language Arts to as a 7th grader the previous year, climbed up to where I was perched at the highest point in the bleachers and sat with me. She didn't want to play because no one was allowing her to have her way with the basketball. We talked about some random things at first. Then, she began to reminisce about her 7th grade school year and how much she liked my class. She asked, "Ms. Ussin, why did you start teaching dance?" I don't even remember the answer I gave, but it was in that moment that I really began to tune into the conversation. I'd forgotten that it was okay to actually have those— conversations—with my students.

I couldn't return the question and ask her why she started teaching dance, but I was able to ask why she felt like she had to have her way on the court with eight other people who were actually trying to play together. When I asked that, the lid came off! I quickly learned it wasn't about not being able to have her way at all. It was about her friend wanting to play with other friends on another team instead of wanting to be on a team with her. That went into a 15-20-minute talk about what she and her friend do on the weekends and who spends nights at whose house and why she was so frequently late to school and literally everything else connected to her and that friend that she considered to be more than a friend. That friend, she revealed, was actually her girlfriend. Because we were genuinely connecting, she shared with me how much she liked her girlfriend and how she gets upset when the girl doesn't act like her girlfriend at school. We bonded, and it made all the difference later in my classroom.

Let me backtrack for a moment.

When I taught this student in 7th grade, she was absent more than she was present because she was suspended just that much. I couldn't believe when she'd said earlier that she enjoyed my class because I didn't have very many memories of her even being there. When she was present, she was in trouble for something. We didn't have much interaction that I could remember. In 8th grade, she was so focused on being with her friends that class proceedings were the least of her concerns. She came to class, and some days she'd participate. Most days, not. If her friends dressed out for dance instruction, she did. If they didn't, she didn't. Sometimes her friends would dress out and participate, but she wouldn't. She was never disrespectful, but she definitely didn't care. After that talk she and I had, though, and the hug I gave her before I sent her back to the gym floor to join in where they invited her, I knew things would change, and they did. Not only was she participating, but she was encouraging her girlfriend and the other girls to participate.

When she learned that the class would be participating in the school's Christmas program and maybe doing an opening performance at the end-of-year 8th grade dance, she wanted to be seen, but she also, in her words, "didn't want to make Ms. Ussin look bad" because now we had a relationship.

The Closing / Lesson Wrap-Up

After that encounter, I reminded myself, going forward, to be intentional about doing in my dance classes exactly what I'd done in my Language Arts classes. I needed to build relationships with all of my students. I needed to connect with them so I could get back to my love for dance and take them there with me.

Change didn't happen overnight, but the school year definitely ended differently from the way it had begun. I had students who actually started to appreciate dance because love and appreciation was exuding from me. I was more patient because I was taking time to learn them as people while learning them as dancers. The children wanted to talk to me more and engage more in class sessions because I actually cared about who they were. Relationships made all the difference, and it taught me that no matter where I am, if I'm not first connecting with the people who are there to learn from me, they won't be learning a thing. They won't open up to me as much as they would if we first connected in some way. They would care about what I know if they knew I cared.

Here is what I suggest for building relationships with your students:

1. Start Week 1! Get to know who your students are and what they like, and connect. (Use interest surveys, "About Me" projects, info games, learning styles surveys, etc.)

2. Be genuine. Have conversations and really listen. They're little people, but they're people just the same. They want to be heard.

3. Make it your business to know something about every student in your class that could spark a conversation at any moment.

4. Listen to the conversations they have with each other and watch their interaction. Take note.

5. Be you, and let them know you too. Share only as needed. If you're being you, this happens organically.

6. Some students want to know you and connect with you simply because they see your connection with other students. This is key! Don't miss the opportunity to pull a student in who took a little longer to warm up to you. Sometimes they need to know, through others they already trust, that it's safe to connect with you.

The Experts Agree

Developing rapport with your students is easy if you are honest, sincere, and genuine with them.

The Teacher's Guide to Success, 2008
Dr. Ellen L. Kronowitz

When teachers engage in meaningful dialogue and talk with students about their interests, hopes, families, opinions—and when they appropriately disclose personal information about their own lives—it sends a strong message of caring and lets the student know that he or she is important. A relationship-driven teacher takes advantage of every interaction with students to build positive and personal relationships.

Relationship-Driven Classroom Management:
Strategies that Promote Student Motivation, 2003
John M. Vitto

Students everywhere need to enter into an important partnership with their teachers. The personal link between teacher and student is essential for successful learning and for a class climate geared to self-discipline.

Discipline Survival Guide for the Secondary Teacher, 2011
Julia G. Thompson

Homework

List at least five different, specific ways you can begin intentionally building relationships with your students during the first week of school. Remember, it's important to plan, plan, plan. You'll thank yourself for having done this.

Chapter 10

Start Strong
Finish Strong

In the classroom, how you start is just as important as how you finish. Not starting strong could cause you to quit before the finish.

-**Ms. Ussin**

The Warm-Up / Bell Ringer

Do you remember my reference in Chapter 5 to the teacher I credit as one of the most influential in my career, the one who said she didn't smile with her students until Christmas? It turns out she wouldn't be the only teacher I would hear say that. I heard it several times throughout my first few years, and if you've been a teacher even one month, I'm willing to bet you've heard it too. Again, these teachers weren't saying we shouldn't smile with our students. That would be unrealistic and, quite frankly, unnecessary and vile. They weren't saying we shouldn't have fun with our students. What they were saying, though, is that it's necessary for a teacher to go into his/her classroom on Day One and firmly establish the order for the classroom that is expected to persist throughout the school year.

Students should know, on Day One, that the classroom is, and will be, a place for learning and growth, and though there may be fun activities to facilitate learning, the classroom is not a playground. It's important for a teacher to make clear who the authority figure is in the room and not only explain rituals and routines, but also demonstrate and practice them. Teachers should make classroom rules clear and rewards and consequences for following or not following those rules even clearer. And most importantly, once all has been set in place, the teacher must stand firm and remain consistent in maintaining every order, every rule, and every expectation. Otherwise, disaster is inevitable, and a playground is likely to ensue. The start matters! It will determine if you'll even be able to finish strong.

Work Session, Part 1: Ms. Ussin's Suggestion

Take the time not only to read through the following list, but also to complete it and check everything off as done before starting your next school year. These are things that should be covered with your students on Day One, or at least during the first week of school. Other questions are sure to arise as you work through this list. Write those questions in the Homework section.

1. How will students enter your classroom each day?
2. Will students have assigned seats? If not, how will seating be determined?
3. Will your seating change based on the activities for the day? How will students know where to sit?
4. Will students be expected to begin working on a bell ringer or warm-up upon entering the classroom? If not, what is the expectation for them upon entering the classroom?
5. What is the required location for all book bags when students enter the room?
6. Are there consequences if book bags and other belongings are not in a particular place?
7. Will students be allowed to write in pencil in your class? What is the pencil sharpening procedure? What are the consequences if the procedure is not followed?
8. How will students dispose of their trash in your class? What is the procedure?
9. Will students be allowed to get up at any time to get tissue, hand sanitizer, etc.?
10. What is the procedure for using the restroom?

11. Will students walk assignments to you when they're done? Will they submit the assignments to a particular place in the classroom? What is the procedure?

12. Is there a particular way you want them to write a heading on their papers?

13. If students finish an assignment before others are done, what will they do while they wait on the others to finish?

14. In keeping with your district's and school's policy on the use of technology in class, what will the procedure for technology use be in your class? Will students have to drop their technology at the door on days when it's not in use, or can it remain on their person?

15. When technology is no longer in use after an activity is done, will students be required to place their devices in the "Off" position?

16. Will there be a designated drop-off station in your class for cell phones?

17. If your district/school does not have a Bring Your Own Technology (BYOT) policy, what is the procedure for unauthorized technology use in your classroom that is in accordance with your district's/school's policy?

18. Will you have group leaders for activities? How will leaders be determined? What other jobs will be assigned in groups? How will students know what their jobs entail?

19. What is the homework policy?

20. How will students be expected to exit your room? Are they allowed to leave when the bell sounds, or should they wait for you to dismiss them?

21. What is the expectation for your students when you travel as a class together in the hallway? How will you exit the classroom?

How will you travel? How will you enter into the final destination? How will you re-enter the classroom?

22. What, in all of this, is necessary to be printed in your class syllabus? On your class website?

23. What are your classroom ground rules?

    a. Is eating allowed in your classroom?

    b. How will students be expected to treat one another? You?

    c. Are there any areas in the classroom that are off limits to students?

    d. Do students need always to raise their hands to speak, or are there times when that's not necessary? If so, when are those times?

    e. Are students allowed to leave their seats at any time?

    f. Are students allowed to talk during presentations (student, teacher, guest)?

24. Will you have classroom assistants: president, office runner, roll caller, etc.? What will their responsibilities be? Will students hold the positions for the whole school year? Will there be an election?

25. What are your classroom disciplinary procedures? What are punishable offenses? What behaviors simply warrant a warning?

26. What will be the Step 1 Consequence? Step 2? Step 3?

27. Will you have a student self-serve station with a stapler, hole puncher, sharpener, tissues, hand sanitizer, etc.? If so, what are the procedures for accessing that station?

28. Will you have set procedures for how students should work in groups? Will specific tasks be assigned to the first member of the group? The second? And so forth? What are the tasks?

29. Keeping your school's fire drill and tornado drill procedures in mind, what will be your specific classroom guidelines for these drills?
30. Keeping your school's lockdown procedure in mind, what will be your specific classroom guidelines for a lockdown?

There could be 100 more questions added to this list! Again, these are to get you thinking, and as you're answering them and planning for your year, other questions will naturally arise. Answer them! Plan, plan, plan! You'll be glad you did. Every detail matters for a strong start.

Work Session, Part 2: Ms. Ussin's Story

The incomparable, educator extraordinaire, Ron Clark, wrote a New York Times Best Seller titled *The Essential 55* that I highly recommend for beginning teachers. The book is a compilation of 55 rules and practices that, after implementation over time, through trial and error, became the very things that made Clark the award-winning teacher and leader in education he is. His practices also allowed him, as the subtitle of his book reads, to discover the successful student in every child. Every rule he details in the book is noteworthy, but there is one that has always stuck with me. When I read it, it reminded me so much of a couple of my own examples.

Clark's Essential Rule 9 reads: "Always say thank you when I give you something. If you do not say it within three seconds after receiving the item, I will take it back. There is no excuse for not showing appreciation."

Clark admitted that establishing this rule was easy. Maintaining it, however, was more challenging than he anticipated. In teaching his students the importance of being kind and appreciative, he would reward them with small gifts and treats for their achievements and accomplishments. Most students would say "thank you" immediately upon receiving their rewards. There were those, however, who didn't, of course. Every time a student didn't say "thank you" within the three seconds after receiving something from Mr. Clark, he, as promised, would take it back and keep it moving. There were times, he explained, that it broke his heart to have to do it, but "they knew it was a rule, and I had stated explicitly the way it worked from day one." Because of this, his students rarely complained about the rule. In fact, they even helped Mr. Clark enforce the rule when they noticed a fellow classmate hadn't said "thank you" immediately. One such case was with a little girl who, along with a few others, won a set of books for having the highest score on a test. The girl was so excited at receiving the books that she jumped up and down with glee. Her classmates pointed out that she hadn't said "thank you," though, and Mr. Clark had to take the set of books back.

Heart-wrenching! For her and for Mr. Clark. But it was a rule, and the rule was the rule.

It had to be upheld.

Sure Mr. Clark wanted to ease up and let the kid have the books, and in other instances he detailed in the book, he would've liked to just forget the rule and let his students have the rewards, but the respect would've gone down the drain and everything he'd worked so hard to build would've come crashing down right before his eyes. He wanted to teach them how to appreciate when someone does something for them, and if the lesson was to be learned, he couldn't let up.

In my English class, I required students to write only in ink on any assignment that would be submitted to me for a grade or feedback of any kind. I didn't accept work that was written in pencil. I explained every year, on Day One, that nothing in professional work settings or in the "real world" is accepted as final when written in pencil. I explained how pencil could be erased and changed. I told them that when applying for jobs or signing documents to purchase a home, ink is what seals the deal. Not pencil. And my athletes always sat up with squared shoulders and wide eyes at attention when I reminded them that they wouldn't be allowed to sign a contract in pencil to play on any professional team.

My students and my parents knew pen only was the expectation. My syllabus and class website detailed that work written in pencil would be returned to be redone and resubmitted in ink. Naturally, I had to return many papers throughout the years because middle schoolers will be middle schoolers. I had some complaints from students when I would return the work to them, but for the most part, students just did what was expected—they would redo the work in ink and resubmit. In my class, as was the case in Mr. Clark's, if students saw their classmates doing the opposite of what was prescribed in the rule, they called it out. If a student was writing in pencil and a classmate pointed it out, they would stop working and start over in ink.

There were times when I hated this practice because some days, students just didn't have pens. They would ask their classmates, and classmates wouldn't have any extra pens for them to borrow. Then, they'd ask me. Most times I would be able to supply them with pens, but there were some rare occasions when I couldn't. This song and dance would waste so much of the student's work time. I would feel bad and almost allow them to just write in pencil, but if I had, I, like Mr. Clark, knew the respect would've gone down the drain and everything I'd worked so hard to build would've come crashing down right before my eyes. I wanted to teach them the importance of professionalism and how some standard practices in our world are just that—standard—if we like it or not. If they were to learn the lesson, I couldn't let up. And I didn't until my 14th school year.

As I mentioned, this rule gave me headaches some days. My students would be consistent in following the rule at the beginning of the school year, but as we approached Christmas break, they'd get lazy and write with whatever they had. They didn't go the extra mile anymore to make sure they had ink pens for class. That school year, as the newness wore off of our days, and students got "comfortable," some wrote in pencil and submitted assignments. Sometimes I would return the work to be redone in ink, and other times I wouldn't, and because I wasn't consistent, I met my own demise.

How was I going to enforce using only ink on assignments for the rest of the year if I allowed a few students to write in pencil on that one assignment in November? I wasn't! I couldn't! It was a done deal the moment I eased off the rule. You better believe, that school year, I got more work submitted in pencil than I had in all of my career. I started strong with the rule, but I didn't follow through and uphold it. I loathed reading work in pencil, but I'd brought it on myself. There was no way I was going to try to start over with them, either. I wasn't going to make some grand announcement and tell them we need to begin again. Nope. I allowed myself to live through the woes of not being consistent, and I'm glad I did so I could have this example to share with you. I've experienced starting strong and finishing strong with the pencil rule and every other rule and practice I had in place. I've also suffered the devastating brunt of the blow that comes with starting but not finishing strong, with the pencil rule and other guidelines.

The Closing / Lesson Wrap-Up

Teacher, you hold the key. Students will respect you and your classroom all the more when they see concrete systems in place and when they know they're held to a standard. There's less "push back" when they know what the consequences are and that they've committed the crime that deserves the consequence. If you allow one student to forego a rule, you will have to grant everyone else the same privilege. It will be inevitable. They'll never let you forget how you allowed one child to get away with murder. You'll be seen as unfair from that day forward, and before you know it, because you have no leg to stand on, your classroom is no longer yours. It's their playground. Those little people will become a unified army against you if they see you've bent the rule for one student and won't bend it for everyone else. Or, they'll be a mighty militia for you when they see you're consistent and don't show partiality. They will enforce your rules for you with their classmates, and you won't have to say a word. You saw it in Mr. Clark's example. You saw it in mine.

No matter how badly it hurts…no matter how you may have to cry (when you get home)…no matter how much they hate you (which never lasts forever, trust me), they'll be okay, and they'll be much better because someone stood firm with them. These are the students who come back years later to thank you for being hard on them and helping them to grow in discipline.

Consistency is key, just as it is with anything in life. Working out for two weeks and quitting for two months isn't the way to see results with your body. Practicing a couple of days a week for one hour with hopes of competing in the Olympics isn't the way to get the gold. Starting strong by enforcing rules but falling off on them in the middle of the school year is a setup for failure. Don't just start strong. Maintain throughout so you can finish strong too.

The Experts Agree

Teachers set the tone for the year on the very first day. The students should experience a routine sequence of activities from the outset.

The Teacher's Guide to Success, 2008
Dr. Ellen L. Kronowitz

Most students realize that discipline is necessary to keep order in a classroom. In fact, some of them are even desperate for order and discipline at school because they have none at home. So, in many cases, they will actually welcome a good classroom management plan. Students want to feel respected just like teachers do. A fair classroom management plan that does not simply rely on anger and intimidation from the teacher is a welcome addition for students as well as teachers.

Discipline without Anger:
A New Style of Classroom Management, 2012
Doug Campbell (the Discipline Doctor)

Great teachers establish clear expectations at the start of the year and follow them consistently as the year progresses.

What Great Teachers Do Differently:
17 Things That Matter Most, 2012
Dr. Todd Whitaker

Homework

What other questions surfaced as you worked through the list? Write them below.

_____

_____

_____

_____

_____

_____

_____

_____

_____

_____

_____

Chapter 11

Rituals, Routines, and All the Foundational Things

The most successful classes are those where the teacher has a clear idea of what is expected from the students and the students know what the teacher expects from them.

-Harry Wong

The Warm-Up / Bell Ringer

In the last chapter, we addressed some of the classroom order questions that every teacher should completely exhaust before ever receiving a student. Starting strong is key. In addition to a strong start, it's imperative for the teacher to institute and maintain well-defined classroom rituals and routines for students to follow all school year for a guaranteed strong finish.

In this chapter, I'd like to invite you into my classroom and walk you through what the first three days of my school year look like—how I set order and establish a strong start, and how I not only introduce students to and explain the classroom rituals and routines, but also how I demonstrate them. As far as I'm concerned, nothing else matters the first few days of school. We have all year to teach. We don't have all year to set order.

Work Session: Ms. Ussin's Story

1st Day of School

On the first day, desks are in rows in my classroom with the seats facing the front of the room. I don't move desks into tables until later in the week or at the top of the second week. This is for a couple of different reasons. 1.) I don't want students in communicable seating because I need their forward-facing, undivided attention at all times. If they're seated in tables, they won't give me their full attention; they'll be focused on each other. 2.) I have to teach students how I want them to communicate and operate when they're seated four to a table. Tables are purposeful, where every student has a specific job to contribute to an assignment or table activity. Day One is not the day to explain how to work at tables; there are too many other important "must do's" to cover that day.

- As I stand at my door to receive students on the first day, I tell them to sit wherever they like. For a moment, they think I'm the cool teacher. Ha!
- Once the bell rings to signify the start of the day, I walk in, close the door behind me and say, *"Good morning to you!"* Usually, the class replies with, *"Good Morning."* Right then, before morning announcements interrupt me, I teach them the first ritual in my classroom. I explain to them that when I say, *"Good morning to you,"* the proper response is, *"Good morning to **you**."* We try it a few times. By then, announcements are on.
- When morning announcements begin, it never fails, because they've been doing this all their school lives, students stand for the Pledge of Allegiance and honor the flag without my having to say so. They are also pin-drop silent during the announcements, which is what I expect. When announcements are over, I explain that whenever there's a voice coming from the overhead speaker, even if I or one of them is midsentence during our instructional period, everything stops. I tell them no one talks when someone is speaking on the intercom. Then, I commend them for doing what I expect of them without my even having to say so. (At this point, I've already started praising them and telling them who they are: principled, respectful students. More on this in the BONUS Chapter.)
- From there, I explain to the students that their choosing a seat was just for the moment. I tell them the plan was for them to sit there only for the announcements. After their shock, and for

some, their disappointment, I tell them that there is a particular way we file into the seats when they're arranged in rows. I say, *"So, let's line up outside of the classroom so I can show you how to properly enter the room and find your seat. Grab all of your things and line up on the wall outside of the room."* Before I walk out, I make sure my Promethean board has the class pledge displayed.

- Once we're all in the hallway, I take that opportunity to explain that there will be times we have to work in the hallway for group activities, scavenger hunts, and station work. I point to each classroom and say, *"There are classes in session. They should never even know we're in the hallway. We're always respectful of the learning environment. The same way we don't want anyone disturbing our learning, we don't disturb theirs. Does everyone understand that?"* I wait for a response of *"Yes, ma'am,"* and if that's not the response I get, I keep asking if I'm understood until students catch on and I hear everyone, in unison, saying, *"Yes, ma'am."* I won't accept just *"Yes."*

- I go on to say, *"I'm not in the habit of repeating myself, especially not with mature middle schoolers, so you all have said you understand, so I won't be addressing this anymore. Are we clear?"* I, again, wait for my *"Yes, ma'am"* response. I won't accept just *"Yes."* About 99% of the time, students already have it at this point.

- After that, I position myself at the classroom door, standing sideways with one foot inside the classroom, and one foot outside in the hallway, facing the line of students before me. I direct the first student into the classroom, telling him/her to go to the last seat on Row #6, which, when entering the room from the hallway, is the furthermost row in the room, clear across the room from the door. Then, I allow the next three students to file in and direct them to simply follow the student before them. The first student sits in the last seat on the row. The second student sits in the seat in front of that student, the second to last seat. The third student sits in the seat in front of the second student, and the fourth student sits in the first seat on the row, the seat in front of the second student. So, basically, the students file in from the back to the front of the row, or from the bottom to the top of the row. Then, I have the next four students file into the next row in the same manner, and I follow this pattern until the classroom is filled from the furthermost row to the row closest to the door.

- Once the class is seated, I say, *"This is the procedure. We do not skip seats. We file in from the back of the row to the top of the row, no questions asked, no matter how we're standing in line, and no matter if 'I don't like where I'm sitting.' This is the procedure. Is that clear?"* By this time, students know the only response I accept is, *"Yes, ma'am."* I wait for it.

- Then, I explain that the aisles are to always be clear. I tell them I walk a lot and that if they have to walk, there should be no opportunity for them to trip over book bags and such. I explain my strict "book bags under the seat" policy and that it's for everyone's safety. Then, I tell my first joke. I say, *"If I ever trip over a book bag or anything else of yours, I'm suing your family."* I tell them I love them, but if I have to be hospitalized because of their carelessness with a safety precaution they said they understood, I'm going to love them and still take their family's money. Students begin to shuffle and make sure everything is neatly tucked under their seats so the aisles are clear.

- I then point to our class pledge that's up on the Promethean board. I teach them the pledge that I did with every one of my classes all but one year of my teaching career. I explain to them that after we greet each other, they are to immediately stand so we can recite the pledge together. Of course, after saying that, it's time to practice.

- I step to the door and open it. I act as if I'm talking to another teacher in the hallway and encouraging students to get to class. The students usually find this funny. Then, I walk in, close the door, and say, *"Good morning to you!"* They say, *"Good morning to you,"* and everyone immediately stands. We recite the pledge and then the students take their seats.

- Next, I point to the board and change to a screen that has the date at the top and a warm-up activity ready for students to complete. I tell them that when they enter the room and take their seats, without question, they are to read the screen and do what it says. I explain to them that they will work on the daily warm-up while I'm at the door clearing the hallway; they won't wait on me to come into the classroom to start the warm-up.

- I say, *"The screen always has the date, so you never have to ask the date, and if you happen to miss the date on screen, you can always look at the calendar here (I point to the calendar on the wall). There will also always be instructions on the warm-up. It tells you exactly what to do."*

- At that moment, I ask for a volunteer to read the warm-up instructions. After the student reads, I say, *"Does everyone understand what you have to do with this warm-up? I've had students not understand before, so I want to make sure everyone knows what's expected. I will gladly explain if you need me to."*

- I take care of any questions and then say, "*Okay. So, now I want you to show me what you're going to do tomorrow when you come into my class. We are going to walk back out into the hallway, but I want you to scramble in line so you're not next to the same people. I have to make sure you know how to file in, no matter where you are in line. This may be our last time practicing today, and it may not. Let's gather our things and head back into the hallway. Before we do that, though, can someone remind me of what I said about how we behave when we're in the hallway?*"

- A student will explain, and I make sure, again, that everyone knows the expectation. Students quietly walk into the hallway and scramble into a line by the door. I position myself at the door and welcome them in. Usually, this is done perfectly. There will always be a class, however, that takes more than that one time. When that happens, I just keep repeating the file in until it's right. This is too important to skip.

- Once students are in their seats, they take out their notebooks or a sheet of paper, whatever they're using that day, put their belongings neatly under their desks with my silent walk through the rows being their reminder, and they start the warm-up activity. When I see all students are set with paper and a writing utensil and that their belongings are completely out of the aisles, I walk to the door and stand just as I would in the morning to clear the halls and encourage students to get to their classes. I pretend, again, to be talking to teachers and students, and my students laugh. When a minute's up, I walk in, close the door, and say, "*Good morning to you.*" They respond with, "*Good morning to **you**.*" I change the screen so students can see the pledge. We recite the pledge, students sit down, I change the screen back to the warm-up, and start the Promethean board timer for 15 minutes. (I always make the first-day warm-up 15 minutes so I can take a breather and gather myself to push through the rest of the class period.)

- As the students work on the warm-up, I start passing out first-day things: student information forms, health cards, agendas, Code of Conduct booklets, and whatever else. Students know not to do anything to those items because the final instructions on the warm-up say: *"Do not do anything with the papers Ms. Ussin brings to your desk until she tells you to do so."*

- When the timer chimes, it's time for me to teach students three classroom routines all at once: (1) how to present in my class, (2) how to submit papers in my class, and (3) how to handle row leader responsibilities.

- For the warm-up, students had five questions to answer about themselves. They were responsible for answering each question in no less than two sentences and completely restating the question in their answer. (With the warm-up, I'm assessing students' ability to follow instructions, their ability to properly form an answer to a question, which is major in ELA, and I'm learning about and getting to know them to lay foundation for relationships.)

- I don't call on any students on Day One. I always ask for volunteers. I don't know them, and they don't know me, so I don't want to cross anyone's comfort level lines. I identify the excited go-getters on Day One, and with that, I'm already learning who will probably be spokespeople for group presentations and other speaking opportunities.

- I try to get two to three students to answer each question so students can see enough presentation in action to understand what's expected. Students are required to stand where they are to share their answers with the class. I explain that with every presentation to the class, they are to stand. I highlight things that are done correctly, and if there's anything a student didn't do correctly in the warm-up, I gently lead the student to understand what s/he did wrong.

- After we've heard from everyone, I tell students to pass their papers up to the top of their row. Once all papers are up, I draw everyone's attention to one of the row leaders as I stand at his/her desk. I say, *"Now, whenever you're a row leader, because you will be at some point or another, you have some major responsibilities. You have to know how many people are on your row, and you must count the papers you have to make sure you have a paper for every person on your row. Next, you must make sure there is a name, date, and assignment title on every paper. If you have a paper or papers that don't have all required pieces, you need to pass the paper(s) back. You will not get up out of your seat and walk papers to anyone on your row. You will simply pass the paper(s)."*

- I then go through the stack of papers from the row where I stand. With the row leader, I examine each paper. If the stack is in order, I have that row stand at their seats and take a bow while the rest of the class applauds. (I had expectations that they met, and I get excited about that. I praise them publicly, and I praise them loudly. More on this in the BONUS Chapter.) If the stack still needs work, I give the stack back to the row leader so s/he can do what the row leader is supposed to do. I go to another row to see if I can use it as the example.

- Once any redos have been completed, I have the rows pass the papers back up. Then, I walk to a different row and demonstrate with another row leader how to stack the papers, making sure all papers are facing the same direction, with names facing up. If paper was ripped out of a spiral notebook, row leaders have a choice with that paper: They can cut the fringes off themselves, or they can send it back to the owner for that person to remove the fringes. I do not accept papers with fringes.

- Once papers are in order, I walk across the front of the room and collect the stacks of papers from each row leader. I say, *"I hope everyone was paying attention and knows the responsibility of the row leader. It could be your turn tomorrow."*

- Next, we walk through all first-day papers, step by step, together. I stress the importance of not getting ahead of me so everything can be done correctly. I walk the aisles the entire time we're going through the papers so I can monitor how students are completing the paperwork. During this time, we also cover some of the topics in the Board of Education's Code of Conduct manual. The principal usually has a schedule for specific topics to be reviewed daily until all has been covered. When all is done, I collect anything that needs to be filed with me or left with the front office and instruct the students to put away anything that needs to be taken home to be signed by a guardian.

- Finally, we walk through the classroom expectations. I don't call them rules. I do this through a PowerPoint presentation titled "All Things Ms. Ussin!" I use pictures and videos throughout to show and tell students who I am and to ensure students understand what they will and will not do in the classroom. It is extremely interactive with a lot of call and response and repeating after me. There are lots of laughs worked into the presentation for the students to loosen up a bit.

- By the end of the presentation, my students know I don't eat broccoli, they know I have a cat phobia, they know I'm an author who loves to read and write, and they know I'm an entrepreneur who runs a dance school. They also know that they don't just get up and walk around the room; they have to raise their hands to be recognized. They know we keep all our trash until the end of class; they don't just get up and walk to the garbage can. And they know what it means to respect each other, Ms. Ussin, and our learning space. They are fully aware of what I expect and what they can expect of me.

- After the presentation, there is a six-question Pop Quiz. Yup, on the first day! But every student aces it! It's simply a recap of what was presented in the expectations PowerPoint. It's multiple choice and almost impossible to fail. This gives me an opportunity to take them through passing up papers again and allows the row leader to get more practice. This also boosts students' confidence, knowing they aced an assignment on the first day. I make sure to celebrate that with my excitement on Day Two. I commend them for paying attention and comprehending what I presented. I usually say something like, *"If this is how y'all pay attention and ace an assignment on the first day and you just met me, I can only imagine how awesome you're gonna be when I really start teaching you."* Whenever an opportunity presents itself, I praise my students to the high heavens!

- It's usually time to switch to the next class by then, but if class is not over by then, I have students scramble in the hallway and file in one last time. We recite the pledge, and I put up a new screen with a five-minute warm-up for students to complete. This warm-up stays in the students' notebooks. I do not collect it.

- To end class, I have students take out their new school-issued agendas and write down homework. I explain to them that this is what we do at the end of each class. I pull up the homework screen and students write: *Get all important papers signed and return them to school tomorrow.*

- When the bell rings for students to go to their next class, I say, *"Don't move. The bell is to let everyone in the building know that the school is in transition, but my class is dismissed with my voice by rows or tables. Does everyone understand that?"* I wait for my *"Yes, ma'am"* response.

- I then dismiss two rows at a time so there's not a stampede. And already, because of how orderly they're required to enter the classroom, they know I expect the dismissal to be done in an orderly fashion as well.

All four of my classes follow this same agenda on Day One.

2nd Day of School

- As students approach my classroom, I greet them. They walk in and file into their seats as they were taught to do on Day One. If a class gets it wrong, you guessed it. I have them line up outside of the classroom and try again.

- There is a screen up on the Promethean board with the date and the warm-up. Above the date and warm-up is a line that says, *"Remember, we read the screen and do exactly what it says."*

- Students take out their notebooks and writing utensils and get to work. Most of the students remember to have all of their belongings under their desks. For the one or two who don't remember, they're reminded when they see other students snatching book bags, folders, and binders from the aisles and tucking them in their rightful place.

- When the tardy bell rings, I walk into the classroom and say, *"Good morning to you!"* They say, *"Good morning to **you**."* As a reminder, I use both hands to gesture, like a choir director, that it's time for them to stand. Some classes need the reminder, some don't, but it is just the second day of school, so I remind them anyway. I change the screen so they can recite the pledge with me. After the pledge, students take their seats and continue with the warm-up.

- After students complete the warm-up, we review it. Then, I pass back their warm-up from Day One, the five questions they had to answer about themselves. I'm intentional about writing something on every child's paper because it's important to me that they know I'm listening to them. If I assign it, they need feedback. On most papers, I simply say, *"Nice to meet you,"* and on some papers, where the answers to their questions call for more of a personal response from me, I write more.

- Next, I have the students take out any signed papers they returned and put them at the top right-hand corner of their desks so I can walk through the aisles and pick them up. Because I need them to stay organized and because there's some personal information on the papers, I don't want them passed up to the top of the row.

- We, then, take the time to review the required sections of the Board of Education's Code of Conduct.

- I pass out the syllabus next. Since there is so much official school business to take care of on Day One, I always save my syllabus for Day Two. We walk through the syllabus and talk about everything they'll be learning, what they need for the class, and when their first project is due. I say, *"We will actually be starting the project today."* They usually look like deer caught in headlights, and it's always the funniest thing to me!

- The last section in the syllabus is the Class Expectations section, which we covered in great detail on Day One with my PowerPoint. When we get to this section of the syllabus, I pass back the students' quizzes from the previous day. Once I've passed back every quiz, we review it alongside the classroom expectations in the syllabus so just in case anyone got anything wrong (very rare), they can see the right answer. This is my time to celebrate the passing scores on the quiz and remind students how excited I am to teach them. I say, *"Y'all are smart! You learn quickly too! I can't wait to get into our stories and writing because I already know we're gon' have a good time. Y'all are already making A's. THIS is how you start the school year!"* Again, every chance I get to applaud students, I take it. Encouragement builds self-efficacy.

- After we review the syllabus, I tell students, *"Have your parent or guardian use the QR code on the back of the last sheet or visit the website listed beneath the code to complete a form for me. The form has some questions for them to answer about themselves, and some for them to answer about you. If your parent or guardian completes the form by Friday (or whatever day fits best for what I'm doing), you will get five points added to your project that we're starting today."* I then direct students to put their syllabi in their notebooks.

- Next, I have students complete a Learning Style Survey and explain to them that this is the first part of their project. The survey has 20 questions. I set the timer for 20 minutes.

- When students are done, I pull up a screen on the Promethean board that shows them how to tally their scores based on the points they received for their answers to each question. I walk through the aisles to help them and to make sure they're tallying correctly. Once they have their final scores, I pull up the next screen that shows, based on their score, if they are auditory learners, visual learners, or kinesthetic learners.

- As I'm walking through, I give each student a sticky note and tell them to wait for instruction before doing anything with it. Once everyone has a sticky note, and I see that everyone has identified the type of learner they are, I say, *"With an ink pen, write your name and your score on the sticky note."* I call each row and have students place their sticky note on either the Auditory, Visual, or Kinesthetic poster on the wall, based on the score they received from the survey. These posters are for me. It informs my instruction for each class. If I have a high percentage of visual learners, for example, I know my presentations need lots of pictures, videos, charts, and other visually appealing teaching tools.

- I tell students, *"So, today, you identified the way you most prefer to learn, but I want you to remember one thing: Just because this is the way you prefer to learn, it doesn't mean it's the only way you can learn. Don't box yourself into thinking you can't learn any other way. You're gonna surprise yourself this year and see that some things you actually learn better with another learning style."*

- Students are instructed to keep their surveys. I then pass out the guidelines for the *Who Am I? Project* that's due a week from the day it's assigned. We discuss the guidelines, in great detail. The project has a grammar portion that allows me to see their understanding and application of basic grammar rules; it has a writing portion that allows me to see if they understand writing structures; it has a portion where they get to express through art on the project poster or verbally on presentation day. Every part of the project requires them to tell me about them in some way or another, and it draws from the questions on the Learning Style Survey. After we dissect the project guidelines, I entertain any questions students may have.

- For the remainder of the class period, students have a worksheet that walks them through the first part of the project—the writing portion. They work quietly at their desks on that guided sheet.

- Five minutes before class ends, I call their attention to the Promethean board. I pull up the homework screen and students take out their agendas. They write down homework.

- Homework: (1) Remind parents to use the QR Code or visit the website. (2) Return any signed papers. (3) Be sure to bring ELA Notebook and dividers to class tomorrow; we will label and organize our notebooks together. (4) Complete the first portion of the project.

Again, this is the procedure I follow for all four of my classes.

3rd Day of School

- By Day Three, students are experts on walking into the classroom and filing into the rows. They walk in, take their seats, and get started on the warm-up. When I walk in and greet them, they respond with the proper greeting and stand. It's a beautiful thing to see them walk through the classroom rituals and routines without having to be told.

- After we recite the pledge that they've almost memorized by Day Three, students grab their seats and continue the warm-up.
- When the warm-up is complete, we review it together. I then tell the students, *"Okay. I need you to take today's warm-up and your warm-ups from yesterday and the day before and put them to the side. We're about to organize our notebooks, and your warm-ups will go into the warm-up section in your notebook. Go ahead and take out your dividers, your loose leaf paper, your notebook, if it isn't already out, and an ink pen."* I also have these instructions on the Promethean board.
- I grab my model notebook and show students, first, how their notebooks should look. Then, step by step, I tell students how to label each of the five sections of their notebooks. The sections are also numbered and listed on the board. I tell students which sections need loose leaf paper and which sections do not. Students who do not have their notebooks in class that day are required to write down the titles of each section and any corresponding instructions for each section so they can organize their notebooks at home. I tell them there won't be another time in class when we walk through notebook organization again.
- After we're done with the organization, students put their warm-ups in the Warm-Up Section, and I tell them to locate their day one Pop Quiz and put it in the Graded Papers Section. After that, we put notebooks away.

152

- Next, we complete the last day of Code of Conduct review. Then, I say, *"Take out your agendas and last night's homework— your writing portion for the Who Am I? Project. Make sure you've filled in your name, date, and class period in the appropriate places. Once that's done, pass your papers to the top of the row. Row leaders, you know your job. Make sure you do it well."*

- While papers are being passed to the front of the class, I pull the Homework screen up on the Promethean board. Students copy their homework from the screen. As students are finishing copying the homework screen, I walk to the front of the classroom and collect homework from each of the row leaders.

- To end class on Day Three, I teach students the fire drill and lockdown procedures for my classroom, explaining the importance of readiness, seriousness, and swiftness. This takes us to the bell that announces the change of class. After students are back in their seats, I dismiss two rows at a time, my standard procedure.

The Closing / Lesson Wrap-Up

There are routines in my actual instruction, routines in how I dismiss my last class of the day, routines with my lunch class for leaving to go to the cafeteria, how to conduct oneself while there, and how to return back to class from the cafeteria. There are rituals and routines for literally everything. The more accustomed students are to systems, the less likelihood of the classroom becoming a playground. When they get set in those rituals and routines the first three days of school, they're looking to operate in them every day. In their minds, the way they learned is THE way, and that's how it should be. I start strong. I have to keep strong throughout so I can finish strong, doing the very same thing at the end that I did in the beginning. And you have to too! The day you decide to break routine is the day you put the first nail in your coffin. Look for the playground that's likely soon to follow.

The Experts Agree

Orderly procedures facilitate the smoother operation of all activities within the classroom.

The Teacher's Guide to Success, 2008
Dr. Ellen L. Kronowitz

Students are more receptive to change on the first day of school than at any other time of the year because they don't have solidified expectations. Take advantage of this opportunity by thoroughly explaining each routine and ritual so students can completely understand your behavioral expectations. It's more important to have students master each behavioral expectation you present than to speed through as much content as you can.

Checklist: Establish classroom management, routines, and rituals with students in the first few weeks of school, August 2019
Dr. Chandra Williams, Founder
Center for Student Achievement Solutions
www.csas.co

At the beginning of the term, establish a few simple procedures for routine classroom activities and then spend a sufficient amount of time teaching these procedures to your students. The extra time you spend teaching your students how you want them to perform these procedures will reward you with saved class time, less confusion, comfortable students, more efficient learning, and a marked decrease in discipline problems.

Discipline Survival Guide for the Secondary Teacher, 2011
Julia G. Thompson

Homework

Have you thought through your first day of school? Have you "ordered your steps" from the beginning to the end of your day? If you have, great! If you haven't, it's worth your time to do so. Even if you need this to start the second semester or a summer session, take the time to think through how you'll proceed when you have the opportunity to start fresh with your students.

Chapter 12

Lesson Plan Leverage

Teacher planning is the thread that weaves the curriculum, or the what of teaching, with the instruction, or the how of teaching. The classroom is a highly interactive and demanding place. Planning provides for some measure of order in an uncertain and changing environment.

-H. Jerome Freiberg and Amy Driscoll

The Warm-Up / Bell Ringer

The most effective classroom management plan is an engaging, impactful lesson plan. Your lesson plan is your leverage. If your daily instructional procedures are scripted to have your children actively engaged in meaningful, matters-to-them-in-some-way work from the start of your class to the very end, and executed as such, your students will be too focused to act foolish. There's less likelihood of your classroom becoming a playground.

The Work Session: Ms. Ussin's Story

Remember Mr. Redfield from Chapter 3? The first week of school, he took time to implement the rituals and routines he established for his class. He gained the students' respect, and he had their attention, but by the second week of school, he'd lost it all. Often, in our weekly team meetings, Mr. Redfield would disclose what was happening in his classes. A few times, he expressed his frustrations that stemmed from having more class time than he had lessons and activities to fill. He spoke of his inability to "keep them busy" the entire class period, no matter what he tried. This meant the children were left with idle time to do what? Turn that classroom into a playground! And that's exactly what they did. Because there weren't enough engaging lessons planned with rigorous and challenging activities, the students "checked out," and they never returned.

I learned, first hand, year one of my teaching career, that if my students' brains aren't busy every second, a Mr. Redfield-type World War III could break out at any time. I saw that I needed to account for every moment, from bell to bell, and every new teacher I meet, I tell them the same.

The Closing / Lesson Wrap Up

Allow me to sum up this way:

1. Know your curriculum and your students' needs.
2. Plan thoroughly to have the curriculum meet your students' needs.
3. Plan according to your students' interests and learning styles.
4. Plan to have them meaningfully engaged from bell to bell.

The End.

Next chapter.

Turn the page.

The Experts Agree

Thorough and well-formulated planning will help you cut down on potential disruptions. If your planning allows for every student to succeed, you are maximizing your chances for effective discipline. Plan worthwhile and meaningful activities to cut down on behavioral problems.

The Teacher's Guide to Success, 2008
Dr. Ellen L. Kronowitz

It is not difficult to recognize classrooms that are alive with purposeful activities and exude a feeling that "there's important work going on here." Students are engaged in their work. The teacher is a facilitator. It is the result of careful and precise planning by the teacher. Nor is it difficult to recognize classrooms where learning has little direction. Students are off task and lack a sense of purpose. There is little evidence of careful and precise planning for instruction.

Powerful Lesson Planning: Every Teacher's Guide to
Effective Instruction, 2006
Dr. Janice Skowron

I've observed over my career in education (both as a teacher and an administrator) that the teachers who have the most student behavioral problems, and the worst classroom management skills, are usually the teachers who deliver the poorest quality of instruction. The quality of instruction is poor because there is a lack of thought and planning put into the lessons.

Classroom Management: A Guide for Urban School Teachers, 2012
Sean B. Yisrael

Homework

Think back to your junior high/middle school days. Do you remember a lesson one of your teachers taught that piqued your interest and maybe caused you to do further independent exploration on the topic? What about high school? What was the lesson(s)? Write everything you remember.

_____

_____

_____

_____

_____

_____

_____

_____

_____

_____

_____

_____

_____

Chapter 13

Keep Learning Keep Growing

Unless you try to do something beyond what you have already mastered, you will never grow.

-**Ronald E. Osborn**

The Warm-Up / Bell Ringer

Know this: Our students will run circles around us in this technologically advanced world that they very much control if we don't keep up with what's going on out there.

Did you hear what I said?

This generation of students is completely enamored with electronics. There isn't much that they're not doing on their phones right from the palm of their hands. Thankfully, education is changing to meet students where they are with the development of electronic books, interactive websites, and apps that can be used in the classroom. School districts are even understanding the need for BYOT (Bring Your Own Technology) so students can be engaged with technology in the classroom. Now, more than ever before, schools are equipped with electronic devices designed for students' personal in-class use (laptops, iPads, etc.). Education is doing its part in making the change. Are you up to speed?

It's easy to step into your classroom the first year and emulate the teachers whose classes you loved when you were in school. It's quite common, actually. If you've already completed your first year of teaching, you know what I mean. Naturally, we connect to and mimic positive, effective examples we've encountered with hopes of others sharing in our experience and walking away with the same satisfaction we did. Those examples, though, no matter how impactful they were for us, may not be as effective today. And that takes us right back to where we started: Education is evolving. Will you?

Teachers should never stop learning to teach. Educators need continual education in order to continue educating. Students' success depends on it. So, a few quick, practical questions:

- Have you already gained access to the online textbook for your course and incorporated instruction and activities from the book into your lesson plans?
- What are some supplemental websites your students can use to brush up on concepts and practice skills you will teach in the classroom?
- Are you already planning to include BYOT opportunities in your lessons so students can use their cell phones for actual academic tasks rather than for making Snapchat videos and texting one another?
- Have you any plans to attend a professional learning session or conference outside of what your school mandates?

Don't cheat your students out of a well-rounded, up-to-date, fresh, and exciting classroom experience. You don't know all there is to know. Study. Research. Ask questions. Connect with other educators. Do the necessary work to give your students what they need.

Work Session: Ms. Ussin's Story

Throughout my time as a classroom teacher, from my very first day, I ran a business outside of school—Praise Movement School of Dance, Inc.—so my time was carefully divided to ensure equal dedication to work, Praise Movement, and home. I didn't want anything to go lacking. In those early years, the business was fairly new and wasn't requiring much of my attention, but as it grew and demanded more of my energy, I found myself being pulled in its direction more regularly to nurture the growth. I became masterfully strategic and intentional with how I structured my days, maximizing my planning periods during the school day so I could do more at school and take less work home in the evenings. There was a span of time, maybe about two solid school years, when I didn't have time to do anything school-related outside of school. In that season of my career, the thought of going to any professional development on my own time was pretty much nonexistent. But that wasn't always the case.

Not only was I attending workshops and conferences before Praise Movement's upsurge (and again when things leveled out), but I was facilitating and presenting at many of them. I understood the importance of getting away and being refreshed and seeing what other teachers were doing. I was well aware that there were new developments in education, because there always are. I wanted to know what was fresh off the press and how I could incorporate the newness into my instruction. If I wasn't learning, I knew I wasn't growing, and if I wasn't growing, my students wouldn't either. Their advancement was contingent upon mine. Sadly, I saw this firsthand when my refusal to prioritize my gifted students' needs almost choked the life out of their joy for learning.

That school year, my principal, an amazing, forward-thinking leader, explained why, at the suggestion of the Instructional Leadership Team, the administrative staff would be restructuring the school schedule. The master plan was to keep our gifted students from being pulled out of their core classes two times a week to attend gifted "sessions" with one of the few certified gifted specialists in the district who were sparsely spread across every school in the county. Students were missing needful instruction and, as many of them explained, not necessarily gaining anything useful from the gifted sessions. Because of the school's uncommonly large population of gifted students, it made sense to build classes of only gifted students (or mostly in some cases) so they could get the intentional, gifted-focused instruction they required. This meant every teacher in the building would need to be gifted certified.

My principal strongly suggested that every teacher complete a nine- to twelve-month course for the certification. The course was being offered by a local educational service agency, a staple in our region that has served the county and several other surrounding counties for decades. I knew it would be a high-quality, challenging course that would sharpen my skills and adequately prepare me to meet my students' needs the following school year. My principal's desire to arm us with more qualifying credentials, I fully understood. My life, however, as I explained, was on steroids.

During the school year, classes for the gifted certification were offered in the evenings and on weekends, the times I devoted to nurturing my business. In the summer, although it would seem I'd have more time to devote to the classes since school was out, I actually had less time. Summer was, and still is, the busiest time for Praise Movement. We kick into high gear at the end of May for our summer dance camp and don't come down until mid-July. I just couldn't see how I'd fit the classes in, and if I'm honest, I didn't even want to see if I could. My plate was already just about full. I told myself adding one more thing would be gluttonous and bad for my health. I selfishly barely even gave it a thought when my principal expressed the importance of this huge step for the life of the school.

I began to rationalize and pridefully remind myself that I'd taken undergraduate and graduate courses that focused on teaching the gifted child, and that even if I'd taken that last class more than five years prior, I'd be fine. I was an innovative teacher, for God's sake! I could just reach back to some old assignments or skim an old textbook and freshen up on a few things to prepare for the one gifted class I was scheduled to teach. I'd taught gifted students before, hadn't I?

I didn't sign up for the section of the course that would begin in January. I didn't sign up for the section of the course that would begin in May. I completed that school year, went into an intense Praise Movement summer, and returned the following year, ready to teach students the state standards, by way of our district pacing guide, with the suggested gifted curriculum that came from the administrative team. Sure, years of experience in the classroom prepared me to be able to teach any curriculum, but there was something missing. I didn't have the extra hands-on experience and depth of study that was offered in the certification course. I was missing the instruction that came from those who not only know what gifted students need, but how to get them what they need. My expertise would only get me so far.

For the first couple months of school, my gifted students, all 22 of them, loved everything about my class. Every day, we were having a ball in that learning environment! Rich discussion, high performance on quizzes and tests, and major creativity with presentations. Then, things changed. The students weren't as enthused about literary discussion anymore. They weren't excited about the group activities that they had once asked for on a weekly basis. It was like pulling teeth getting them to do anything, really. They weren't disrespectful, and they would do what they were instructed to do, but the joy that would usually accompany their movement about the classroom was no more.

I prayed and asked God to show me what was happening with that class and why things had changed so drastically. I needed guidance; I didn't want to lose them. I also talked to one of my teammates who was enrolled in the gifted certification course, and as I explained what I saw happening with the students, the answer to the question I'd asked God came through her. My teammate helped me see that I was teaching my gifted students the same way I was teaching all of my other classes, and that was the crux of the problem. Hadn't the gifted students been pulled out to have a class all their own for a reason? They learn differently! Hadn't I been commissioned to receive training for tailoring instruction to their needs? Had I accepted the commission, I would've been reminded that gifted students need assignments and activities that allow them to be independent, with guidance only as necessary from the teacher. I would've learned that tiered assignments, creative problem solving, and project-based instruction is key. They didn't need a hands-on, heavy-on-the-instruction teacher. They needed a facilitator of learning, one who would allow them to learn through exploration and discovery. I had to hop into gear, study up, and meet their needs, or run the risk of losing them, which could have all been avoided had I simply remembered that I should not stop learning. I should not stop growing. It was my responsibility to stay fresh for my students, and I failed. Don't let my story be yours too.

The Closing / Lesson Wrap-Up

Again, if you're not learning, you're not growing, and if you're not growing, the students aren't either. It is your duty to take your state's standards and create interactive, engaging ways for students to meet and exceed those standards. You are obligated to know what's new in education and implement it into your instruction. If you're not doing that, look for a playground.

- **Read books that teach you about teaching.** (You're reading a good one now!) Teachers fight for personal down time, I know, but even committing to a chapter a day, or even a chapter a week is better than not reading at all.

- **Listen to podcasts or audiobooks that teach you about teaching** if getting your hands on a hard copy and sitting still with it is out of the question.
- **Attend workshops and conferences beyond what's required by your district.** May I be frank? You need workshops and conferences. This is where the real learning and growth takes place. Workshops and conferences are designed to specifically target teacher needs, whatever the need. (See Homework.)
- **Sharpen your delivery skills,** and resharpen as often as necessary.
- **Develop a variety of ways to present different concepts.** When those delivery methods get stale, revamp and start all over again.
- As much as possible, **incorporate technology in meaningful, impactful ways.** May I be frank again? Your students need it. That's it. They absolutely need it.
- Teaching is a profession where collaboration is necessary. If you're out there alone, you'll drown. **Connect with other teachers on social media.** I met some of my favorite #teacherfriends on social media. There are beautiful, budding, encouraging teacher communities on Facebook, Instagram, and Twitter. Join the fun! I'd love to connect with you. (@msussinteaches)

Keep learning; keep growing. Your students' lives depend on it.

The Experts Agree

The knowledge humans possess is expanding so rapidly that the infrastructure of knowledge has to be continually adapted to accommodate new insights and understandings. Thus teachers, like their students, are faced with needing to learn constantly just to keep abreast.

Instruction: A Models Approach, 2007
Mary Alice Gunter,
Thomas H. Estes, &
Susan L. Mintz

Great teachers have a plan and purpose for everything they do. If plans don't work out the way they had envisioned, they reflect on what they could have done differently and adjust accordingly.

What Great Teachers Do Differently:
17 Things That Matter Most, 2012
Dr. Todd Whitaker

Effective leaders are persistently in search of ways to improve, grow, and strengthen. Teachers need opportunities to rejuvenate, revalidate, and recommit to their profession. They take every afforded chance to increase their skills and knowledge.

If You Don't Feed the Teachers, They Eat the Students!
A Guide for Administrators and Teachers, 2010
Dr. Neila A. Connors

Homework

Do a Google search for **Education Conferences 20____**. Find a few that interest you and that you believe offer sessions that can help you grow. Commit to going to at least one this school year. Talk to your administrator about having the school fund your registration fee. Sometimes, when your principal or assistant principal sees the benefit of your attending the conference, they'll fund it, as money is set aside in school budgets for teacher development.

List your conferences below.

P.O.W.E.R.
Teaching Tools

If you've been to any workshops I've facilitated or any conferences where I've presented, you've surely heard me break down the P.O.W.E.R. Teaching Tools or at least refer to them. And if you've followed me on any social media platform for any time, you've seen and heard the P.O.W.E.R. Teaching Tools there. Not much is different here except me explaining it all in writing. So, if either of these descriptions fit you, this chapter is perfect to skim for a refresher.

If you've never heard me speak, you don't want to miss the gems in this chapter. *(And why haven't you heard me speak? You're missing out on a good time! Ha! See the last page in this book so you can get me to your district for professional development!)* My P.O.W.E.R. Teaching Tools presentations are always magnetic. We have the best time! But more than anything, teachers, principals, and other school leaders rave about how practical the tools are and how necessary they are for new teachers.

Why P.O.W.E.R.?

The P.O.W.E.R. Teaching Tools could have been called anything. Why P.O.W.E.R., though? Why do the teaching tools have to be *P.O.W.E.R.* Teaching Tools? Well, if we define what power tools are, we'll better understand why the teaching tools are called P.O.W.E.R. Teaching Tools.

Good ole' Wikipedia defines power tools as "tools that are actuated by an additional power source and mechanism other than the solely manual labor used with hand tools." We're familiar with power tools. One example is a drill. Rather than using a screwdriver to do work, a carpenter or contractor or anyone who would need to use a screwdriver could use a drill that is actuated by a motor for its power. They'd get the job done more efficiently, and in most cases, more effectively.

The same is true for a chainsaw when it comes to taking down a tree. One could use an ax instead, but wouldn't it be faster, more efficient, and more effective to use a motorized tool for such a huge task? A no-brainer, right? Power tools have the advantage over hand tools, and it's the power that makes the difference. Likewise, in the classroom, it will be the P.O.W.E.R. that sets your class apart.

Keeping in line with the definition of power tools, let's look at a definition I developed for P.O.W.E.R. Teaching Tools—"tools that are actuated by student needs rather than solely by administrative mandates, state and district curriculum, and state testing." When teachers are activated by student needs, their instructional strategies have P.O.W.E.R., they manage their classrooms with P.O.W.E.R., and they build meaningful, lasting relationships with their students with P.O.W.E.R. Any teacher can step foot in a classroom with regular tools and execute instruction, but only teachers who are driven by student needs operate with P.O.W.E.R.

When motivated by student needs and implemented with wholehearted intention, fidelity, and consistency, the P.O.W.E.R. Teaching Tools are 100% effective for managing a classroom. The teacher is the "motor" that ignites the power, though, so offering only a fraction of effort will cause the tools to be unprofitable and result in wasted time and maybe even frustration.

Finally, each of the P.O.W.E.R. Teaching Tools works in tandem. A teacher can't execute just the P. and W. tools and not include the O. and E. and R. tools. The power won't materialize like that. Proper use of every one of the tools is necessary for maximum power in instruction and classroom management, and for building positive, meaningful relationships with students. They all have to work together for the teacher to have a classroom and not a playground.

Shall we take a closer look at each of the tools you'll need to operate in power?

What are the P.O.W. E.R. Teaching Tools?

Passion

I don't know about you, but when I'm seated in a theater, watching a stage play, I'm drawn in by the thespians who exude passion in their performances. Sometimes, too, when I'm just watching TV at home or catching a blockbuster hit at the movie theater, I can't help giving all of my attention to the actors and actresses who "steal the show" with realistic portrayals of the characters they play. There's nothing more exhilarating than seeing artists who love what they do step outside of themselves, completely embody their characters, and give 100% of their zeal to the viewers from the beginning to the end of the show. It's certainly more enjoyable than watching performers who just go through the motions. And for any student, being in the classroom with a passionate teacher is more enjoyable than being in the classroom with a teacher who isn't. You know it's true, don't you? Think about it. You had passionate teachers in school who made you fall in love with whatever they were teaching, even if you didn't like the subject. Or was that just me?

Am I the only one who dreaded History until my senior year in high school because it wasn't until then that I finally had a teacher who loved what he taught and taught his students to love it too? Did I endure all those years in school simply attending my History classes because they were required? Yes, I did, hating every day of it. I came alive, however, when the beloved Mr. William Bryant changed everything. His passion gave me an appreciation for History that has beautifully enriched my adult life. There was no question when I became a teacher that I'd be zealous like Mr. Bryant. I wanted my students to love what I was teaching because I loved it. I wanted them to take what I was teaching and use it in their lives.

You also had teachers who almost caused you to lose your excitement for subjects you loved, didn't you? I know. I did too. I enjoyed Math almost as much as English in school, but when I got that one teacher who thought she could teach Math from behind her desk, my "Math joy" was obliterated for a time. That teacher showed up to class every day, as I said, expecting to sit at her desk and tend to personal business like writing checks for her bills and addressing and stamping the envelopes for those bills to be mailed later. She was a coach for one of the spirit teams at our school, so she sometimes spent entire class periods sewing hems on skirts and making hair bows for the team for Friday night football games. She'd assign work from the Math book with no explanation and would encourage us to collaborate with our neighbors to basically figure things out on our own. I remember very little Math instruction from her that year, and whenever she did stand before us to teach, it looked painful. It never seemed that she actually wanted to teach us. We were her chore, and that was unmistakably apparent. I felt cheated (because I was). There was no question when I became a teacher that I'd do and be the exact opposite of her. Again, I wanted my students to enjoy what I was teaching them. I knew they would need to see my fervor if they were to be ignited. Your students will need the same. If you expect to teach with power, it can't happen without passion.

Praise

Every school year, without fail, of my four classes, I would always have one class that needed to be encouraged more than the others to sharpen the skills they'd need to perform on and above grade level. I'd usually have one class, too, that was rowdier than the others and needed encouragement to be more respectful or less disruptive. With each class, no matter their deficits, I played on their strengths and praised them to the high hilts for any and every strength that revealed itself, no matter how big or small!

I would be on pins and needles every year for the first few weeks of school to see where each class shined. As soon as I knew where each class exceled, I made it known. I put my foot on the gas and never let up. I learned that there's power in praise! It's a tool that every teacher should use daily, and consistently throughout each day. I'm a firm believer that we can speak things into existence because I've seen it played out in my classroom every school year. When I told my students who they were, and I continually praised them for being who I said they were, they became who I said they were. Every time. I called them who I wanted them to be.

Let me explain.

One school year, my 1st period class was the class that had the highest percentage of students consistently completing homework. It seemed like a trivial thing, especially because more and more teachers were choosing not to assign homework. I didn't care if homework wasn't as big a deal anymore; I knew it was something I could use to motivate that class to do more than just homework. I decided to start calling them *Ms. Ussin's Finishers*. I would remind them every day that no other class had as many students completing homework assignments as they did. I would say, "I'm sure it won't be long before you start outperforming other classes with their classwork because you're taking the time to actually complete practice assignments for homework." And do you know what happened? They did exactly what I said they would. They began to run circles around the other classes because I praised their strengths and told them they would perform better than the other classes because of that strength. Because I spoke it into existence, the seed was planted in their hearts. They believed it, and they eventually achieved it. This "speaking things into existence" was a regular occurrence in my classes, every year.

I praised loudly. I praised publicly. I praised often.

Let me say that again.

I praised loudly. I praised publicly. I praised often.

And I did so with every class for whatever their strength (or strengths) was.

What Are Some Ways to Praise Students?

1. **Write individual notes to students.** Do this on sticky notes, on formal stationery paper or a special card with an envelope, with Dry Erase marker on the student's desk, or any other way that will personalize your message to the student. I have former students who are now adults that still have notes I wrote them when they were in 6th, 7th or 8th grade. Every one of them expressed how the note stayed with them because it encouraged them. There was power in that praise! Most of the notes were no more than two to three sentences, but whatever I wanted more of from my students, I praised it, and 100% of the time, I got what I wanted.

2. **Write whole group notes to a team of students or an entire class.** These are really fun! Have a "love note" of praise posted on the Promethean board/Smart Board for them when they enter your class. In the middle of your lesson, pull up a screen with a video you made just for them. Write a note to them on chart paper and hang it outside of your classroom for the whole world to see. Type up a generic message to a class team or an entire class, have copies made, and write students' names on them. Pass them out at the top of class and watch how beautifully the rest of the class period goes. Group notes have power!

3. **Add "shout outs" for individual students or whole classes to the morning and/or afternoon announcements.** When the whole school hears you praising your students, it's a game changer! After your words about them have been spoken schoolwide, not only does it plant the seed in your students' hearts that they are who you say they are, but they're now aware that the whole school is watching to see them live up to it. It creates a drive and tenacity in them to "keep the crown." They don't want to be anything but who you say they are, and in that, there's power! Eventually, they're not working to please you anymore. They start working hard and setting and achieving goals for themselves, becoming exactly who you say they are.

4. **Hand out certificates and homework passes like candy.** Give certificates and/or homework passes for good behavior, homework completion, highest test score, best manners, most caring, most daring, most improved, good try... What am I saying here? Find a reason to praise your students to encourage

them to do more! Award them with certificates so they'll have something in their hands to commemorate the moment. Make a ceremony of it every Friday or every Monday, whatever floats your boat. Game! Changer! Talk about power!

5. **E-mail and/or call parents and brag on their children.** Sadly, teachers have a bad rep for contacting parents only to report the negative. Why not change the narrative and write e-mails and make phone calls to let parents know how well their children are doing? If you're a parent, you know there's nothing sweeter than hearing good news about your children. Be the catalyst for parents' joy when they learn that their children are "doing them proud." I have students who visit me years after they have left my class and remind me of messages I sent to their parents. I have parents who do this too. A few parents remind me, every time I see them, how an e-mail I wrote or a note I sent home still makes their hearts smile and, in some cases, how it completely positively changed their children's view of teachers and school.

Who among us doesn't walk a little taller when someone pats us on our backs with encouraging words…when someone tells us "Good job!"… when someone lets us know they believe in us, while watching and cheering us on to continue doing well? There's so much power in praise! Your students need it. Don't let this teaching tool go unused.

Own It

Own what? Own your uniqueness. You are the main teaching tool in your classroom because you're the teacher. You set all other tools in motion. And just as was detailed in *Chapter 1: Are You Being You?* and *Chapter 8: Be You,* your students don't want you to try to be like another teacher. They want you. *(If you happened to skip right to this BONUS Chapter because you learned of the P.O.W.E.R. Teaching Tools and wanted to read up on them first, no judgement. Do what you do. I would, however, go back and read Chapters 1 and 8 to better understand what it means to own your uniqueness.)*

Rapper Chuck D. said, "Before people buy from you, they have to buy into you." This is especially true of students when it comes to connecting with their teachers. Before they can digest, or even hear what you're teaching, they've got to trust you to be the one from whom they should receive. But when they can see that you're authentically you, and you're owning your uniqueness, bringing all of who you are into the classroom, the electricity is activated, and there's no greater power.

World the Work

Students understand that they need Math and Reading classes. They understand why they have to take History, Science, and electives that introduce them to different skills. What they don't understand, though, is why the methods to teach them what they need to know are so outdated. Why are teachers lecturing them for entire class periods and having them take notes? Why are teachers showing them videos from the '80s and '90s? Why are students being made to read chapters from actual hard-copy textbooks and write key terms and questions?

Our world is more technologically driven than it's ever been and will only continue to advance in that respect. Our students live in that world. Education has made many strides in developing electronic, interactive instructional materials, yet teachers aren't fully implementing them into their lessons and activities. And where does that leave the students? Bored. Uninterested. Disengaged. Students need their teachers to world their work. Not only should the curriculum be up to speed with where the world is today, but it should also interest the students and matter in *their* worlds. What we teach should meet our students right where they are.

In *Chapter 12: Lesson Plan Leverage*, I wrote, "If your lessons are scripted to have your children actively engaged in meaningful, matters-to-them-in-some-way work from the start of your class to the very end, and executed as such, your students will be too focused to act foolish. There's less likelihood of your classroom becoming a playground." This is the kind of instruction that has power—instruction that connects to students' lives.

Teachers have the urgent responsibility to know their students and to tailor lessons to who they are and what they need. Shakespeare may be required, but how do we make Shakespeare relevant to this century and matter in their world? Sure, understanding rock formation, corrosion, and erosion is good, but why is it necessary? Why does it matter in their world? Math computation is an essential skill. Students understand that they'll need that to count their money and pay their bills. But why do they need equations and geometry? Make it matter. World their work—all of it—and you'll see power in your classroom like you never have before.

Use what your students are accustomed to. Yes, teach them other ways to learn because not every activity can be done electronically, but make each method equally as engaging and connected to "where they live."

Expectations and Excitement

You will want to put this next sentence in your pocket; it's a nugget. **Students do whatever teachers allow them to do, but they want to do what teachers expect of them.**

Your students want you to set expectations for them, and they *want* to work to meet them. Even the most difficult students step into your classroom on Day One, bright eyed and hopeful, waiting for you to tell them what the year will be like, what you expect of them, and what they can expect from you. They want to please their teachers, and if they know you're looking for "it," and you're excited about seeing them do "it," they'll reach for "it." If you have continual, consistent, and reasonable expectations for your students, they'll actually come to expect your expectations of them. And that's where the power lies. That's when this tool really gets to work!

Think about the people in your life who had a say in your upbringing… the ones who guided you and pushed you to be your best self. These people could be parents, grandparents, aunts, uncles, coaches, mentors, or even teachers. You respected them and considered them important in your life. You didn't want to disappoint them. You knew they wanted the best for you because they poured their time, their resources, and their love into you. What they thought mattered. What they suggested, you considered. You knew they expected you to walk a path that would make them proud, and because of the relationship you had with them, you *wanted* to make them proud. Any time they let you know what they expected of you, you worked hard to meet their expectation; you didn't want to let them down. They excitedly cheered you on, every step of the way, as they watched you work.

Is this not what expectation should look like in the classroom? Shouldn't teachers pour their time, talent, resources, and love into their students and raise the bar on their expectations for them? What will you expect to see from your students daily—academically and socially? Shouldn't you tell them that you want the best for them, show them how to be their best, and then wait to receive their best? That's what they're yearning for! They can't wait to earn the gold sticker you place on papers that show improvement. They expect it because they met your expectation. They can't wait to hear their names called on the intercom during morning announcements for highest team scores all week. They expect it because they met your expectation. There can be a continuous cycle of excited expectation, and there's power in that. You want that power in your classroom.

And don't be afraid to raise the bar on your expectations. If you set the bar high, students rise to reach it. I often tell new teachers, *"You're gonna be amazed at what your students can do if you simply set the bar high with your expectations. You're gonna be surprised, too, how they don't work as hard when you set the bar low."*

I want to leave you with this thought on expectations that comes from the Common English version of the Bible. Proverbs 13:12 says, "Hope delayed makes the heart sick; longing fulfilled is a tree of life."

There will be a classroom full of little hearts, hoping for you to expect of them. If the expectation is never made known, or if it was introduced but never upheld, or even if it's upheld, but there's no genuine excitement in seeing students even meet the expectations, it will make their hearts sick or break their spirits. They won't have anything to reach for, so they'll be likely to not reach much at all. But if they know the expectations, and they know the teacher is cheering them on, excitedly anticipating their success, it's a longing fulfilled, and the proverb says

P.O.W.E.R. TEACHING TOOLS

that's a tree of life. Imagine that life being rooted and growing and growing, producing healthy fruit every day in your classroom!

Relationships

Show me a teacher who has genuine, organic relationships with her students, and I'll show you a teacher who rarely—and I'd venture to say, never—has to deal with major behavior issues. Just as Dr. Creekmur said in the foreword, as I said in *Chapter 9: Build Relationships*, and as every other teacher who's taught at least one year has said—relationships matter! They are everything in the classroom.

Take Ms. Golde, for example. Ms. Golde knows her students. She can usually pinpoint why Jack is having a meltdown and understands that it's not him showing out or intentionally disrupting the class. She's aware he has deficits in reading comprehension and rather than asking for help because he's frustrated, his frustration turns into anger, and a tantrum is the only way he knows how to vent that anger. Ms. Golde knows this is something he does at home because she's knowledgeable about his home life.

Ms. Golde also knows Nema. She knows Nema's regular sleeping in class isn't disrespect. She knows Nema is the eldest of six siblings and responsible for preparing dinner for the family. Nema bathes the youngest two every night and puts them to sleep and then prepares herself for bed. Ms. Golde knows Nema is responsible for waking early enough to get three of her siblings ready for school, making sure they have breakfast, and seeing them onto the school bus because her mom has to be to work before they all awake.

How does this help Ms. Golde? Rather than assuming Jack is, as I said, showing out or being intentionally disruptive, she can talk to him about what she knows is happening. She doesn't call him out in front of the class or make a big deal about it all. Her relationship with him takes the reins. She counsels him on how to express his anger. She reminds him to raise his hand to talk to her about what he's feeling so they can walk through his feelings, and eventually, the assignment, together. If Ms. Golde didn't know Jack, she could've assumed he was acting out to get attention. She could've scolded him for his behavior, which would've only made him angrier, and who knows how things may have escalated from there?

And her relationship with Nema takes the reins too. When Nema sleeps in class, Ms. Golde knows she needs the sleep, so she allows it. Nema is an A student. She works hard on every assignment and even helps other students with their work. Nema would never intentionally put her head down and not pay attention. In fact, if ever Nema missed an assignment, she would beat herself up about it. Ms. Golde knows this. She also knows Nema's bus is usually the first to arrive, so she arranged for Nema to visit her classroom any morning before homeroom to take care of any missed assignments. When Nema sleeps in class, Ms. Golde doesn't have to walk over to her desk to tell her to sit up and run the risk of upsetting her. She doesn't have to make a scene in front of the other students. Her relationship with Nema allows her to keep peace in the room and keep Nema on track academically.

Imagine understanding every student in the classroom this way. It's possible. It's necessary. Make it your business to know at least one thing about every student that could spark a conversation at any time. Let that one thing lead to another thing, and that thing to another. Your students need you to know them. Knowing them and having organic, genuine relationships with them allows you to teach with power.

See *Chapter 9: Build Relationships* for more on student-teacher relationships.

Rituals and Routines

The only reason relationships, rituals, and routines aren't discussed first in this BONUS chapter is because the R comes last in P.O.W.E.R. If we weren't following the order of the acronym, these would have certainly been the leaders of the pack. They are, in my opinion, the most important. Establishing and maintaining positive student-teacher relationships and having solid rituals and routines will take care of the majority of any behavior issues in the classroom. Hands down. I'm a living witness. This is why two chapters—*Chapter 10: Start Strong, Finish Strong* and *Chapter 11: Rituals, Routines, and All the Foundational Things* are dedicated to outlining exactly what teachers should consider and execute in establishing norms in their classrooms.

Rebecca Alber, *Edutopia* Consulting Editor and Instructor at UCLA's Graduate School of Education, said, "Routines and consistency matter greatly and are necessary for creating a smooth learning environment in your classroom. Routines help with creating community, checking for understanding, and managing the classroom."

I wholeheartedly agree.

In her book *Learning to Teach…not just for beginners*, Linda Shalaway explains, "Routines are the backbone of daily classroom life. They facilitate teaching and learning… Routines don't just make your life easier; they save valuable classroom time. And what's most important— efficient routines make it easier for students to learn and achieve more."

Again, I wholeheartedly agree.

"Keep in mind that behavioral expectations and rules are not mean or bad; actually, they are comforting for students. When you outline a detailed classroom management plan, students know exactly how to earn your praise. A consistent plan also lets students feel safe, knowing what to expect when they walk into your classroom each day." Founder of Center for Student Achievement Solutions, Dr. Chandra Williams, hit the nail on the head with this one.

Set systems are your power. Don't relinquish your power by avoiding or completely ignoring the need to constitute rituals and routines.

The P.O.W.E.R. Teaching Tools, again, if implemented completely and used consistently will guarantee a well-managed classroom and lessen the chance of the classroom becoming your students' playground.

Acknowledgements

To my Worker Bees and the Worker Bee Parents, thank you for agreeing to do the cover for *Your Classroom or Their Playground*. You're famous! And you should be after working as hard as you did in the face of a global pandemic. You all never complained and you went the extra mile on every assignment and with every activity. Our days in the classroom could have been doom and gloom, but they were anything but that. We had fun! I pray you'll never forget your teacher. I certainly will never forget you. Y'all better stay in touch! I love you.

Thank you, *Crystal E. Smith Photography, LLC* for capturing the exact vision I had in my heart for the cover. Such a fun session for the kids and me! And you work magic with the lens! I know we started off in a teacher-parent relationship after I taught your genius son, but I know the Lord has more in store for us. This, I know, is only the beginning.

To my former student, Jasmine (@dolled_by_dubbaaaa), you already know I'm not letting anyone else braid my hair because you take the best care of your teacher! No one would know, from looking at the cover of the book, that I'd worn those braids for about four weeks at the time. That's how awesome your work is, every time. Not only did you excel in the classroom when you were my seventh grade student, but you go beyond excellence in your role as a cosmetologist. Thank you for your professionalism, 5-star punctuality, and love. I pray abundant blessings over you and your business. I am so proud of you, and I love you dearly!

Tori (@torinicolethemua), my heart smiles at every thought of you. I remember the student you were—hard working, respectful and thoughtful, always eager to learn, easy going and fun-loving. None of that has changed. You're the same way as an adult in your profession as an MUA and cosmetologist. I have no doubt your business is growing the way it is because of that. You're good to people, and as I've shared with you before, that's "the way" of business...taking care of your people. I've told you on several occasions: I don't want anyone else in Augusta painting my face, and I mean it. You always get me just right! Thank you for taking such great care of your teacher and for always encouraging me in the things God has called me to do. I pray God's favor over you and your business. May you prosper in everything you do. I'm so proud of you! I love you.

Mrs. Hollis, we're two for two. There are quite a few people I could've called on to edit my books, but I just want you. You've been taking care of me since the Louisiana Tech days when I sat in your classes learning the ways of a journalist. I can only hope you'll continue to see about me. It's been such a beautiful ride, don't you think? I'm so grateful for you.

The Author

Ms. Iantha Ussin served in the Richmond County School System in Augusta, GA for 15 years, being repeatedly named a highly qualified middle grades ELA teacher.

Not only was Ms. Ussin instrumental in raising academic achievement for over 2,000 students, but she consistently fostered a well-managed, fun, safe and orderly environment that was conducive to learning for all students.

It's her mission, now, to EDUCATE, EMPOWER, and EQUIP pre-service and new teachers with the same classroom management practices and skills she successfully employed in her own classroom, year after year.

To book Ms. Ussin for professional development sessions, conferences, or keynote addresses, visit www.msussinteaches.com.

Connect with Ms. Ussin on social media at @msussinteaches

Facebook

Instagram

Twitter

LinkedIn

YouTube

CPSIA information can be obtained
at www.ICGtesting.com
Printed in the USA
LVHW101942140622
721276LV00004B/462